Petrarch's
Poetics
and Literary
History

For Susan and Liz

Acknowledgments

Appearances sometimes to the contrary, criticism and scholarship are collaborative activities. I would like to take this opportunity to thank the men and women at Cornell and Yale from whom I have learned and continue to learn what poetry, language, and thought are and are capable of. A Fulbright-Hays Graduate Research Grant allowed me to begin research in Florence in 1973, and Amherst College helped finance work on the later stages of the book. Among others, Stephen Barney, Jackson Cope, Ann Jones, Louise Brown Kennedy, Arthur Kinney, Arthur Marotti, and Edward Mendelson asked the right questions, saw connections, and reinforced my belief that Petrarch's poetry was far from being a dead letter. To Professors Elizabeth Bruss and Jack Cameron of the Amherst College English Department I owe special thanks for their readings of early drafts and their suggestions for revision, as I do also to Professor Timothy Bahti of the Comparative Literature Department at Cornell University. I am grateful to the Wayne State University Press for permission to reprint a revised version of "Historical Theory and Poetic Practice" which first appeared in *CRITICISM*.

Contents

Foreword

The use of the term "literary history" as it appears in my title, and is frequently appealed to in my readings of Petrarch's *Canzoniere* and *Trionfi,* requires some explanation. I will neither be discussing Petrarch's reception—"Petrarchism" in sixteenth- and seventeenth-century European lyric poetry, for example—nor attempting to fit Petrarch into a scheme of historical periodization for which I have found him to be in some part responsible. Instead, the literary historical aspect of my subject involves the literary inter-relationship inscribed in the Petrarchan texts themselves between a notion of the self and its history or story, and an understanding of language which raises problems concerning any and all narrative representations. What I come to address as a "Narcissistic structure" obtaining between subjects and predicates, selves and narratives, highlights the peculiarly non-narrative element which is always operative as well whenever Petrarch enacts the attempt to narrate a story or present a historical view. Petrarch's concept of history vis-à-vis a traditional medieval historical understanding, which I describe as mutually inverse images, suggests the priority that structural issues might take in our coming to terms with what appears to be a significant relative shift in the modes of reading and writing experience, both historical and poetic.

The Petrarchan texts which I discuss locate themselves neither within nor outside of traditional medieval modes of self and narrative understanding, but rather insist upon the priority of poetic relationships in their production of significance and hence in their presentation of poetic tradition or literary history. Consequently, I read Petrarch's Italian poetry in response to, as well as to arrive at an understanding of, certain formal and stylistic features which seem to me motivated by a recognition (or decision) that the signifying possibilities of the medieval "allegorical" mode of discourse (as particularly exemplified by Dante's *Commedia*) are no longer imaginatively available. My study of Petrarch's "poetics," then, involves interpreting these features with a mind toward questions of symbolic systems and literary-historical understanding, rather than offering a characterization of prosody, allusive range, and technical construction in more strictly philological terms.

I
Historical Theory
and
Poetic Practice

*. . . the only way to escape
the prisoner's state is to
know how the prison is
built. . . .*

*. . . we have only to
identify the point where the
imagined fortress does not
coincide with the real one
and then find it.*

*Italo Calvino, "The Count
of Monte Cristo"*

In a seminal article on Petrarch's historiography Theodor Mommsen once argued that Petrarch's division of history into two clearly demarcated epochs—the enlightened classical period and the medieval Dark Ages—represented a radical break with the principles of medieval historiography, and strongly influenced later humanist historians whose concept of history remains in certain respects similar to our own.[1] Petrarch's poetry, John Freccero has more recently speculated, was equally revolutionary vis-à-vis a medieval past, and just as central to the subsequent development of Western European writing.[2] Freccero's discussion of the poetics of the *Canzoniere,* though, while demonstrating brilliantly Petrarch's transformation of Augustinian and Dantesque understandings of moral error into a "new aesthetic," implicitly complicates the question of Petrarch's place or position in literary history. The linguistic principles whose operation in the *Canzoniere* he begins to uncover—the absence of a principle of intelligibility and, in that absence, the impossibility of maintaining the integrity of the signifiers which make up the collection—have a direct bearing on the notions of "history" and "change" in terms of which Petrarch appears to be a pivotal figure.[3] To the extent that Petrarch's poetry appears to play out the destabilization of one theory of language and interpretation, that enacted and elaborated in the "medieval" texts it evokes most persistently, it also threatens to destabilize the writing and reading of literary "tradition" or "history" that constitute our position, the position from which we find this poetry "new."

If we re-examine Petrarch's concept of history in light of Freccero's reading of the *Canzoniere,* we find a similar difficulty in calling this concept radical simply in the sense that it differs from and supersedes a previous concept. By virtue of representing a shift in the interpretation of the past, it, too, poses fundamental questions about any and all such interpretations. Neither historians nor readers of Petrarch's poetry have as yet offered a reading of Petrarch's historiography which takes the problematic status of change itself into account, nor have they sought to establish a more extensive relationship between the understanding of language displayed in Petrarch's Italian poetry and his "modern" presentation of history. Since this kind of inquiry would involve calling into question the commentator's own authority to know or to judge Petrarch's achievement in either field, it is not surprising to find that Petrarch the poet and Petrarch the humanist are customarily kept segregated.[4] Ironically, though, Petrarch's texts are not well served by this reluctance to mix modes. As the following argument is designed to demonstrate, an understanding of language which raises problems concerning narrative representations of experience (such as any "history" must inevitably attempt to be) is displayed by Petrarch's rewriting of history no less than by his poetics, while the poetry takes on a special pertinence when considered in terms of his historical revisionism.

A major obstacle to the kind of understanding I am proposing has been the valorization of Petrarch's representation of history over medieval representations, particularly as the former introduces the concept of historical periods. There is nothing ambiguous, of course, about the condemnation of the contemporary, "medieval" world and its way of looking at things, as expressed in Petrarch's letters and poems. "The natural perversity of the times" and "the sterile-minded wretched men who people it" are castigated by Petrarch the poet and Petrarch the political commentator alike. The standard against which the depravity of his own dark age is measured is always provided by ancient Roman civilization, presented as a distinctly different and far superior epoch. After the fall of his contemporary Cola di Rienzo, the self-proclaimed Roman tribune who was to restore the Roman Republic, there is a shift in the emphasis of Petrarch's praise—to the Roman Empire—but the principle of opposing the degenerate present to an exemplary past is never abandoned.[5] However, the very use of ancient Rome as a paradigm raises a different sort of interpretive problem than that of determining the semantic sense of Petrarch's historical comments. If the model in terms of which all events are to be interpreted is itself derived from a historical event or period (and if that model may be revised at will to suit the circumstances of the historian), then the authority of that model, and of the interpretations of history it generates, are open to question. The apparent circularity of referring to an earlier period in order to establish a notion of periodization, which, in turn, fixes the identity of that earlier period, is symptomatic of certain ahistorical, purely poetic or literary operations, constitutive of the model, which might be described as follows: in order to oppose present and past such that each period may be understood in terms of the other, it is first necessary to mark a division between them which is, then, already constitutive of a difference that the paradigm of Rome only appears to establish. Once this division is made, the significance of the paradigmatic period, no less than that of the period whose negative characteristics the former reveals, is constituted by the relationship between the two. The apparent priority of one over the other, whether conceived of as logical, chronological, or aesthetic, is, then, a kind of optical illusion, the product of a constitutive relationship which escapes the hierarchical arrangement it gives rise to.[6] Petrarch's periodization of history, in other words, might well call our attention to its arbitrariness. Petrarch's statements *about* history are clear enough, but the status of this history is by no means clear.

Accordingly, Petrarchan texts register both exhilaration with the new possibilities of thought and action suggested by an alternative historical vision, and despair over the inadequacy of this "history" as a means of understanding the self and the world. Commentators, though, have seen Petrarch's history as a truer understanding of the course of human events, taking the ambivalence with which it is presented as a sign of Petrarch's disinclination to think systematically, of an indecisive, inconsistent sensibility which did not, however, prevent him from being suddenly clear-sighted where his predecessors had been foolishly blind.[7]

The influential nineteenth-century art historian Jacob Burckhardt is, perhaps, most responsible for the mediated/ unmediated formula in terms of which the difference between Petrarch and his predecessors (or the "Renaissance" and the "Middle Ages") has often been framed. Accepting humanism's myth about the Middle Ages, a myth which Petrarch's texts did much to foster, as if it were empirical fact, Burckhardt informs us that "in the Middle Ages both sides of human consciousness —that which was turned within and that which was turned without—lay as though dreaming or half awake beneath a common veil. The veil was woven of faith, illusion, and childish prepossession, through which the world and history were seen clad in strange hues. . . . It is in Italy that this veil dissolved first; there arose an objective treatment and consideration of the State and of all the things of this world."[8] Burckhardt offers an especially interesting example because, not unlike Petrarch, he was engaged in remapping the past. He is often said to have "invented" the Renaissance much as Petrarch is said to have discovered antiquity. Burckhardt's allegory of the Renaissance, though, unlike Petrarch's representations of ancient Rome, announces his understanding of the historian's task as that of establishing the "objective" meaning of history. While this belief in the possibility of an unmediated, objective, historical account runs counter to, it may also be read in terms of, our present concern with the ahistorical, "poetic" aspect of historical interpretation. In the sense that, as Roland Barthes once put it, history "acts as a sort of psychoanalysis"[9] of the present, Burckhardt's view of the Renaissance might be said to define (and seek to legitimate) a certain outlook on his own situation. Burckhardt's history, too, in other words, displays the priority of an ahistorical interpretive act taking place in the present moment of narrative representation.

Burckhardt's view has remained compelling. One finds repeated as a truism in a recent textbook edition of selections from Petrarch's works that it is "a more vigilant historical sense" that Petrarch "bequeathed to the successive generations of humanism."[10] Such a repetition, however, does not represent even an act of historical positioning like Burckhardt's. It does not perform a reading of, but only lies trapped within, an image of Petrarch the historian whose significance still lay, in Burckhardt's text, in its difference from other images of historical interpretation. The mechanism of such entrapment receives considerable attention in Petrarch's *Trionfi,* where the narrator portrays himself as often blocked by his suppression of the relational aspect of the significance of the historical lessons from which he attempts to learn, and I will have more to say about the consequences of this blockage in my reading of that poem. My point here is that in order to catch a reflection of our own historical thinking in the mirror offered by Petrarch's, it is necessary to assume that his "story" and ours do *not* coincide. To imagine that Petrarch's way of understanding the world is "more vigilant" or less mediated by imaginative structures than that of his immediate predecessors—because it seems to coincide with the subsequent periodizations of history which have become almost second nature to us—is to see oneself only as the object of a historical unfolding rather than as also its subject and author, however problematic this ambivalent position may prove to be.

In the absence of the self-flattering presupposition that Petrarch's view of history represents an advance toward enlightenment and truth, and with the help of a brief structural comparison, it is the congruence of Petrarch's "new" conception of history with the medieval model of universal history which it presumably supersedes that begins to suggest itself. Structurally speaking, Petrarch seems not so much to have invented history as to have inverted it. The identification of the post-classical era as "the Dark Ages," for example, reverses a figure for historical change which, as Mommsen observes, was "not at all new, for throughout the Middle Ages it had been used to contrast the light, which Christ had brought into this world, with the darkness in which the heathen had languished before His time."[11] Similarly, Petrarch's effort to revive classical learning is counterpointed by his determination to bury medieval Christian culture in oblivion. The age of Augustine, Aquinas, and Dante is to be passed over in silence because it is unbearable to be reminded of Rome's fall into the hands of inglorious barbarians.[12] Although he finds it a "peculiar notion," Mommsen concludes that Petrarch's conception of history is epitomized by his rhetorical question, "What else, then, is history, if not the praise of Rome?"[13] Mommsen's realization, accepted so reluctantly by himself, suggests the point to be made about the nearly symmetrical histories of Petrarch and his predecessors. The peculiar notion of history as the praise of Rome bears a strong, if perverse, resemblance to the notion of the medieval historian, which might be epitomized by the question, "What else is history if not the praise of God?" The substitution of Roman glory for Christian redemption as the central event in history appears to govern Petrarch's inversions and to inaugurate not so much the new age of unmediated understanding pictured by Burckhardt, as a subversion from within of the mode of thought that it also counters.

Turning to Saint Augustine, we find that Petrarch's alternative way of interpreting history has in fact already been defined—negatively—by the system against which it has been said to stand. In the *De doctrina cristiana,* where Augustine most fully develops his theory of signification and interpretation, there is a relevant discussion of figurative language. Taking Paul's admonition, "For the letter killeth, but the spirit quickeneth" as the occasion for his exegesis, Augustine illustrates the linguistic commonplace that meaning depends, not upon a simple correspondence between word and thing, but upon the way signs, and presumably the things they signify, can be related to each other with reference to a common center or principle of intelligibility. According to Augustine, a literal interpretation of figurative signs, insofar as it is possible, conceals these relationships and, in so doing, undermines the very faculty of rational thought (so, at any rate, Augustine's analogy between this literal-mindedness and the intellectual capacity of beasts strongly implies):

> . . . when that which is said figuratively is taken as though it were literal, it is understood carnally. Nor can anything more appropriately be called the death of the soul than that condition in which the thing which distinguishes us from beasts, which is the understanding, is subjected to the flesh in pursuit of the letter. He who follows the letter takes figurative expressions as though they were literal and does not refer the things signified to anything else. For example, if he hears of the Sabbath, hc thinks only of

one day out of seven that are repeated in a continuous cycle; and if he hears of Sacrifice, his thoughts do not go beyond the customary victim of the flocks and fruits of the earth. There is a miserable servitude of the spirit in this habit of taking signs for things, so that one is not able to raise the eye of the mind above things that are corporal and created to drink in eternal light.[14]

As Augustine goes on to elaborate, the literalism with which he is concerned is a kind of idolatry.[15] Petrarch recognizes himself as a literal reader of history and knows that in Augustinian terms this is idolatrous. Indeed, idolatry is the metaphor he uses in the *Canzoniere* to describe the autonomous nature of the poetic event, the discontinuity between a poem and any other moment outside or beyond it.

Similarly to Augustine, the French philosopher Jacques Derrida links the principle of coherence with "the concept of a centered system," though with the difference that he does not call this center God or the spirit. He describes the kind of interpretive center or principle of intelligibility required for such a system in functional terms which are appropriate for describing what happens in the absence of such a center as well: ". . . it has always been thought that the center, which is by definition unique, constituted that very thing within a structure which governs the structure, while escaping structurality. . . . The center is at the center of the totality, and yet, since the center does not belong to the totality (is not part of the totality), the totality has its center elsewhere."[16] Augustine's God fulfills these conditions. The coming of Christ, an event which happens within the system of human history but originates elsewhere, epitomizes or makes explicit the divine intention governing all other events, the totality of whose meaning transcends (for Derrida, "escapes") their temporal structure. Ancient Rome, on the other hand, does not fulfill these conditions. As Petrarch conceives of Rome, it is only a part of the totality of history. Even if he could anticipate the preservation of some idea of Rome for the duration of human history, the origin and end of this idea would still be strictly temporal. Because it is located entirely within the system, there is no transcendent reason for privileging the idea of Rome above any other element of the system, and such elevation is necessarily arbitrary. Used as a principle of intelligibility, such an element generates meanings, but the authority or certainty of these meanings is lost. Petrarch's use of ancient Rome as the center of his historical structure functions, in fact, as a decentering of a signifying system (since the nominal center lacks absolute authority) which results in a breakdown of the processes of signification itself. Any sort of integrative, referential process is undermined since the relationships generated between one event or moment and the next appear at best to be mere fictions. Symptomatically, the center itself is represented by Petrarch as an absence. It is simply an empty name. The presence that this name once pointed to is lost, Petrarch continually insists, and only if its ideals and values were revived, could Rome be restored. ("Who can doubt that Rome would rise up again if she but began to know herself?")[17] Once Petrarch's historiography is considered in terms of the issues of signification and interpretation it problematizes, it should come neither as a surprise nor as mere coincidence that his poetics performs a similar function with respect to certain ways of writing and reading poetry. The poetry should provide a further commentary on the writing and reading of history for the same reason—that history is redefined by Petrarch as a literary construct, open to the same possibilities and subject to the same limitations as other literary constructs.

Though there is probably no way finally of answering it, the question of Petrarch's motivation in manipulating systems of signification in this way necessarily remains. It is, after all, his own substitution which alters perspectives in such a way that antique Rome is perceived as an absence. Up to then the medieval world did not consider itself to be discontinuous with antiquity, and therefore could not entertain the possibility that Rome and its Empire had ceased to exist. Why should Petrarch have taken it upon himself to tamper so drastically with a theory of signification which relatively successfully mastered the anxieties of structurality? In retrospect it appears that the pressure of political and cultural conflicts contributed to the breakdown of traditional modes of thought. But the typology of intellectual change remains notoriously elusive in this kind of explanation. Even were the idea of historical determinants not itself problematic, such forces would not necessarily account for the forms through which new ways of organizing experience take shape, as a closer scrutiny of Petrarch's struggle with poetic tradition will illustrate.

To Freccero's description of the *Canzoniere* as a series of lyric "fragments," discontinuous poetic instants "strung together like pearls on an invisible strand," whose juxtaposition does not add up to any structural totality or thematic resolution, we might add that the behavior of Petrarch's language thus displays the syntactic consequences of his reorganization of history.[18] Freccero also reasons that "the lyrics . . . counterfeit a *durée* by their physical proximity and so create a symbolic time, free of the threat of closure," and again, though usually put more negatively, the same could be said of "historical" moments as they constitute and are constituted by Petrarchan historiography.[19] But for Freccero a purely poetic explanation of these strategies suggests itself. The advantage for Petrarch the poet of writing this way is that it runs counter to the way taken by his illustrious predecessor Dante. Petrarch's poetics, Freccero conjectures, manifests what Harold Bloom has called the "anxiety of influence," a poet's fear of being overwhelmed and poetically paralyzed by a predecessor's achievement, and thus his desire to swerve away from and/or subvert the predecessor's powerful example.[20] This account seems consistent in a different way with Petrarch's historiographical strategy. If Petrarch did not discover history, his historical revisionism nevertheless provokes a kind of anxiety of structurality which could make poems as well as the past (in this case the medieval past) appear as intellectual and psychological stumbling blocks. It seems unlikely, though, that a desire for poetic originality would account for the direction of Petrarch's moral and historical writings as well as for his poetics.

A comment by Umberto Eco on the medieval theory of allegory, as it is summed up by Dante in the letter to Can Grande, offers a complementary perspective on Petrarch's relationship to Dante. Eco is speaking of a way of reading Scripture, poetry, and the figurative arts, but, as we have seen, this was also a way of reading history. He writes: "The order of a work of art in this period is a mirror of imperial and theocratic society. The laws governing reading are the laws of an authoritarian regime which guide the individual in his every action, prescribing the ends for him and offering him the means to attain them."[21] What Eco identifies is the relationship of structures of interpretation to structures of social and political organization. Insofar as Petrarch desires changes in the latter, he might also have to become party to changes in the former. Dante seems quite obviously to be the target, the figure to be confuted, in the *Canzoniere,* but the anxiety which, for Petrarch the poet, is condensed in the spectre of Dante, could derive as well from the ideological configuration which Dante must have mirrored so powerfully for his near contemporaries. In fact, the anxiety of influence may always have a more political aspect than Bloom's Freudian model admits of. Thus, we need not deny that Petrarch's poetic originality often takes the shape of a struggle with his precursor Dante, but we need not see his poetry solely in terms of that struggle either.[22]

There is evidence that Petrarch tried to change structures of thought and society without publicly signaling the extent of his ideological subversiveness. Specifically, he does not seem to have had in mind an open break or even a visible conflict with Christianity, except where theology could be used to justify and maintain the secular status quo. Although his scheme of history, for instance, is tantamount to a refutation of the existence of God as Authority or Author in terms of the traditional scheme, Petrarch artfully camouflages this sort of implication in his didactic and polemical writings, though not, as we shall see, in his nonpolemical works. Thus in a gracefully seductive letter addressed to his friend Giovanni Colonna (but later revised and collected for a more public audience in the *Familiares*), the casual reader is protected from the anxiety-producing implications of one of Petrarch's descriptions of Rome. This letter, later passages of which are cited by Mommsen and others as among the clearest expressions of Petrarch's new concept of history, opens by paying lip service, in highly Augustinian language, to the medieval Christian principle of interpretation. Petrarch writes: "We are to read philosophy, poetry, or history in such fashion that the echo of Christ's gospel, by which alone we are wise and happy, may ever be sounding in our hearts,—that gospel, without which the more we have learnt, the more ignorant and wretched shall we be, to which, as the highest citadel of truth, all things must be referred; on which alone, all the firm foundation of sound learning, all human toil is built."[23] In the body of the letter, however, under cover of this conventional formula, Petrarch proceeds to comment upon the places the two friends visited together on their walks through Rome earlier that year in such a way that the echoes of pagan antiquity tend to drown out the echo of Christ's gospel. Not only do the references to sites recalling ancient Roman history far outnumber those to the landmarks of Christian Rome, which he hastens through in two sentences, but an alternative typology quietly usurps the function of the one explicitly posited as the ultimate point of reference. Petrarch's description pays little attention to the actual disposition of historic sites, but follows instead the chronological order of events in Roman history.[24] Later in the letter, when Petrarch exhorts, "Who can doubt that if Rome should commence to know itself, it would rise again," he is urging that Rome see itself, that it constitute its identity, not in terms of salvation history, but in terms of ancient history, since, according to salvation history, Rome's identity remains constant.[25] The device of periodization, paradoxically, is used to obscure the conflict between the two principles of intelligibility. Peaceful coexistence and even complementarity between the two visions of Rome are implied by Petrarch's comment to his former companion that, "we seemed to be divided; you seemed better informed in modern, I in ancient history."[26]

Turning to Petrarch's appropriately titled *Secretum* and the poetry of the *Canzoniere,* we find, on the other hand, a prodigious display of the most far-reaching textual and interpretive disturbances. In the *Secretum,* conflicts and contradictions are thematized by means of an inconclusive dialogue between an erring lover, "Franciscus," and his mentor, "Augustinus." The fiction that this dialogue is intended only for the eyes of its author apparently releases the work from the constraints which might have been imposed on it by short-term social and political responsibilities, and from the beginning it opens upon a vertiginous *mise-en-abîme* of textual uncertainties. The Lady Truth who is said to appear to the author of the dialogue and to guide its writing identifies herself as the Lady Truth depicted in Petrarch's Latin epic, the *Africa.* Were this admission that she is one of his own poetic inventions not cause enough for suspicion, she calls him, in turn, "another Amphion of Thebes" for having built her a beautiful palace in his earlier poem.[27] In Dante's *Inferno,* Thebes is invoked consistently as the type of infernal "society," and implicitly as the antitype of the Heavenly City, the City of God, described by the historical Augustine. This Lady's genealogy is, then, doubly suspicious: she is not simply a poetic character or construct, but the construct of an architect/artist who, in terms of Dante's or Augustine's scheme of things, is himself cut off from (transcendent or absolute) truth. If Truth she nevertheless remains, it is a peculiar truth. The poet instinctively greets her in the words which Vergil's Aeneas addressed to his mother Venus, before he recognized her as his mother, in the woods near Carthage: *O quam te memorem, virgo? namque haud tibi vultus / mortalis, nec vox hominem sonat* (What name could I give you, Oh virgin, for your face is not that of a mortal person nor does your voice have the sound of a mortal voice?).[28] The identification of Petrarch's Lady Truth with the goddess who always appears to her son in a false guise, the goddess of carnal love who never reveals herself as herself until the moment she vanishes, and never allows her son to embrace her, aptly characterizes the ambiguity of language which replaces Augustinian coherence as "truth" in Petrarch's writing. Signifiers are perforce literal, but their significance is hardly for that reason any more tangible, transparent, or otherwise interpretively "graspable" than that of signifiers that operate figuratively.

The reasons why truth has become an inaccessible siren, why Petrarch presents himself in a position vis-à-vis Lady Truth akin to that of Vergil's Aeneas vis-à-vis his mother (and not like that of Dante's pilgrim in his journey toward Beatrice, even though Petrarch's Lady is herself given to echoing Beatrice) are gradually unfolded over the three days of dialogue which follow. On the third day of Franciscus' debate with Augustinus, the latter, a figure introduced through the problematic mediation of "Lady Truth," momentarily crystallizes one of the binds that Petrarchan interpretation and the interpretation of Petrarchan texts find or put themselves in. The kindly father, who has gone out of his way to be accommodating in order to rescue his charge from the long and dangerous spiritual malady which afflicts him, finally loses patience on the subject of Franciscus' love of

Laura. What he claims to object to is not simply that Franciscus loves Laura, but that he loves her in the wrong way. Despite Franciscus' claim that his love of Laura has led him to love God, Augustinus objects that this love inverts the "true order" of love by putting love of the creature before love of the Creator, that, in other words, it is idolatrous. "You have admired the Divine Artificer as though in all His works He had made nothing fairer than the object of your love, although in truth the beauty of the body should be reckoned last of all."[29] Franciscus, implicitly invoking the Augustinian doctrine of letter and spirit, counters that he has loved Laura's soul as much and more than her body, as demonstrated by the fact that his love has survived and even grown stronger as time has lessened the physical beauty of his beloved. Augustinus, suddenly literal-minded and sceptical, then traps Franciscus in what seems to be a self-contradiction:

> *Ag.* Are you kidding me? If the same soul inhabited an ugly and deformed body, would you have loved it as much?
> *Fr.* I do not dare say that; the soul cannot be seen, and the appearance of such a body would not have promised as much; but if the soul were apparent to the eye, I would certainly love its beauty even though it had an ugly home.
> *Ag.* You are appealing to verbal tricks; for if you can love only what appears to the eye, you have therefore loved the body.[30]

The trick, however, can be undone only at Augustinus' expense. If it is the case, as Augustinus suggests in both his question and his response to Franciscus' answer, that the soul is invisible and inaccessible except through its problematic incarnation in the body, then, as he unwittingly implies, the body or corporeal image alone constitutes whatever access the lover may have to knowledge of the incorporeal soul. Theologically this conclusion has grave consequences. In rejecting Franciscus' suggestion that the soul might become apparent via some other means than a strict one-to-one correspondence to the body, he renders meaningless his accusation that Franciscus has put the creature before the Creator, for if the soul can be known only by its body, then by the same representational logic, the Divine Artificer can be known only through His works. That is, if the relationship between creation and the Creator is analogous to that posited here between body and soul, then what is thought of and desired as God must be an extrapolation from the physical universe and the written texts through which He is known. In this case, it makes no difference whether the creature or the Creator comes first. To love Laura is merely to substitute one error, one illusory, idolatrous relationship, for another.

The text does not make these inferences explicit. (It is a further indication of how this text operates that it does not proceed by means of linear argumentation.) Instead it is significant that Augustinus makes no mention of the historical Augustine's doctrine of the spirit and the letter, that he in fact tacitly denies it just at the moment when it could have been invoked as a means of converting Laura into a new Beatrice. Apparently the problem of idolatry would be inherent in any attempt to base knowledge upon representation (which would also involve the logical, hierarchical habits that this text abjures). Without the Augustinian doctrine, on the other hand, the text can neither assert nor deny the truthfulness of either of its interlocutors' exchanges; Franciscus' subsequent appeal to the relationship between letter and spirit in the context of what Augustinus insists is a wholly idolatrous love affair serves to involve the doctrine itself in the indeterminate ironic mode that places both speakers on an equal footing, or rather leaves neither of them any ground at all to stand on.

The text does turn, nevertheless, soon after this series of exchanges, to a display/discussion of two compensatory strategies for establishing some order, some set of priorities in one's life and language. The first is exemplified by Franciscus who, as Augustinus charges, has settled on an arbitrary principle of intelligibility which endows his existence with only a specious, solipsistic coherence:

> . . . who could sufficiently utter his indignation and
> amazement at this insanity of a deranged mind that,
> from the moment you were taken by the splendor of
> her name as well as that of her body, has with incred-

ible conceit venerated everything which appeared in accordance with that name. For this reason you have loved so intensely the laurel, either of emperors or of poets, because both the one and the other are called by this name; and from that time there has issued from your pen only with great difficulty a lyric which makes no mention of the laurel. . . . Finally since you could not hope for the imperial laurel, you have sought the laurel of poetry, which promised you reward for your studies, with no more moderation than that with which you had loved her who was mistress of you.[31]

Franciscus' strategy is not, however, as mad as it seems to Augustinus, as the text's allusion here to an earlier criticism of a still worse case of verbal fetishism helps us appreciate.

In *Inferno* XXXI Dante's Vergil reprimands Nimrod, whose senseless address to Dante the pilgrim and his guide is also called mad:

> *Anima sciocca,*
> *tienti col corno, e con quel ti disfoga*
> *quand'ira o altra passion ti tocca!*
> *Cercati al collo, e troverai la soga*
> *che'l tien legato, o anima confusa,*
> *e vedi lui che 'l gran petto ti doga.*

Stupid soul, keep to your horn and with that vent yourself when rage or other passion takes you. Search at your neck and you will find the belt that holds it tied, O soul confused: See how it lies across your great chest.[32] (*Inf.* XXXI, 70–75)

Then, as if Dante the pilgrim might still be tempted to try to make sense of Nimrod's words, Vergil firmly puts a stop to any conjecture about their meaning:

> *Poi disse a me: "Elli stessi s'accusa;*
> *questi è Nembròt per lo cui mal coto*
> *pur un linguaggio nel mondo non s'usa.*
> *Lasciànlo stare e non parliamo a voto;*

> ché così è a lui ciascun linguaggio
> come 'l suo ad altrui, ch'a nullo è noto."

Then he said to me, "He is his own accuser: this
is Nimrod, through whose ill thought one language
only is not used in the world. Let us leave him
alone and not speak in vain, for every language is to him as his is to others, which is
known to none." (*Inf.* XXXI, 76–81)

Nimrod's horn, Dante's own invention, underscores Vergil's
claim that Nimrod's "language" has no meaning or translation.
It is empty (*voto*) because, although it indicates Nimrod's confusion and stupidity to one who can interpret it correctly, it in
no way escapes such self-referentiality. His "words" are not,
properly speaking, signs at all. Despite its frustratingly suggestive appearance of syntactical and grammatical coherence,
Nimrod's outburst might as well be the unarticulated noise of
a horn blast. The most extreme instance, short of silence, of
blocked and perverted language in *Inferno,* Nimrod's discourse
represents the *reductio ad absurdum* of literal language. The
confusion of tongues for which Nimrod has traditionally been
held accountable is located here, not in the use of different languages (which is merely a symptom of that confusion) but in
the abuse of the very principle of language—namely, that it
must point beyond, not simply to, itself.

Up to a point Franciscus' arbitrarily structured life and
work are analogous to Nimrod's gibberish. The appearance of
syntactical and grammatical coherence in either case dissimulates
the fact that there is nothing to either order but a play of differences and similarities among signifiers (or sounds) themselves.
But they seem to have arrived at their respective situations from
different directions, and we note that for Franciscus the two
images of literal language—Nimrod's nonsense syllables and
his horn blasts—which in Dante's poem could stand for each
other, are no longer equivalent. Where Nimrod's language is
all sameness which he tries to articulate by means of difference,
the *donné* of Franciscus' situation, as Augustinus himself has
implicitly conceded, is that *all* meaning is constituted by an
endless play of the differences and similarities of signs or

sounds themselves. Under this circumstance a horn blast or its equivalent takes on new value. Franciscus' homonymic use of the single term *laura* to link the otherwise unrelated fragments of his existence might be regarded as a reasonable defense against the madness of a discourse not so organized. Though Franciscus' *laura* may be no less empty of significance in the classical, epistemological sense than Nimrod's purely material, nonsignifying horn blast (whose virtue is that it can be seen and heard for what it is), it is no more, and possibly less, absurd than endless, unrecuperated difference. As subtext to the *Secretum*, Nimrod's inability to understand others' discourse and they his when he forgets his horn serves as a warning of what might happen without such a defense.

Franciscus' strategy, however, is only half the story of the *Secretum*. This strategy, which has been to retain the form of the centered system, supplying the center from within, still distresses Augustinus, who insists that the interpretive power with which Franciscus' Laura has become invested is destructive. Augustinus' alternative strategy, formulated to counter the violence that Franciscus' exclusive love does to "the soul" (Augustinus either inconsistently or optimistically retains this category, although he never seeks systematically to establish its status), is to diminish the power of any one signifier to act as an ordering principle, by dispersing this power among several different or successive love objects. Appealing to Ovid as his authority in these deep and decidedly nontheological waters, he recalls the suggestion of ancient philosophers and poets that an old love may be driven out by a new love as one nail is driven out by another:

> Ovid, the master of love, is in agreement with this advice, expounding a general rule that "every love is conquered by a new one that succeeds it." This is undoubtedly so. The divided soul, turned toward many objects turns to each of them with greater slowness. Thus the Ganges, as they say, divided by a king of Persia into many streams of water, from a single, terrible river, was reduced into many brooks of negligible importance. Thus a scattered army becomes pene-

trable to the enemy; thus a fire spread out loses vigor
and all force so that as it grows standing united, it
diminishes when dispersed.[33]

But the diminishment of violence to be hoped for from this dispersal of force, Augustinus foresees, cannot be guaranteed.
Pluralism might become by far the more dangerous course, due
to the possibility that the "lover" might become as fascinated
with each one of several images of coherence as he has become
with one:

> On the other hand, however, it is to be feared that,
> while you escape a nobler passion, if so we may call
> it, you will fall into many others, and from being a
> lover, you will become an inconstant fickle lady's
> man. In my judgment, if it is inevitable to perish, it
> is at least a comfort to perish through a nobler evil.
> You will ask me what I therefore counsel. I do not
> disapprove of taking hold of the soul and fleeing, and
> migrating from one prison to another. Indeed, in
> passing from love to love there may be some hope of
> liberty, or of a less imperious domination. But I do not
> approve of your freeing your neck from a single yoke,
> only to subject it to innumerable different kinds of
> foul slavery.[34]

If the relationship of the signifier to the interpreter does not
change according to the change in the status of the signifier
(and to think it would is probably hopelessly Utopian, Augustinus reluctantly suggests), then the violence done by discourse
to the soul, or the truth, or whatever one thinks of as nonlin-
guistic reality, grows worse with the proliferation of nominally
centered signifying systems. It is noteworthy, on the other hand,
that Augustinus, unlike Franciscus, still dreams of escaping an
epistemological servitude to the letter and is willing to sacrifice
the relative security of Franciscus' strategy to this end.[35]

In the *Canzoniere,* both accuser and accused call themselves "I," but once again the question posed is why the lover
cannot tear himself away from the inadequate principle of intelligibility which he himself, recalling the terminology of the
De doctrina, calls an idol—*L'idolo mio scolpito in vivo lauro*

(My idol sculpted in living laurel [30. 27]).[36] Like Petrarch's comments on the history of the world, his history of the self lacks the ontological grounding, the center, which would allow relationships between events, or even between moments, to emerge. Laura, as the desired center of the lover's existence, manifests the same inadequacies as Rome, taken as the center of human history. She is mortal and she is absent. As in the *Secretum*, no attempt seems to be made to dissimulate the disorder which ensues. In one sonnet, *"Benedetto sia 'l giorno, e 'l mese, e 'l'anno"* (Blessed be the day, the month, and the year [61. 1]), the day on which the lover first saw his beloved is ecstatically memorialized, and in the next, without transition, it is strongly denounced—*"Padre del ciel, dopo i perduti giorni"* (Father of heaven, after the lost days [62. 1]). In the space of one line in the opening sonnet, *Di me medesmo meco mi vergogno* (By me myself I myself am ashamed of myself [1. 11]), the poetic subject itself disintegrates into fragments, doubling and reflecting, but failing to stabilize, each other. Where is the moment of conversion which governs the structure of Augustine's *Confessions* and which the lover recognizes intermittently as the way to redeem the lost days of indeterminacy?

One answer to the question is that Petrarch's method of structuring both public and private history finally precludes any such moment or operation. Only the miracle prayed for in the concluding hymn to the Virgin could bring it about. It is no longer the cause or the effect of reading one's life. In part, at least, this is because once an element like Rome or Laura is taken as the point of reference, and once it is perceived as different or absent from the present, the possibility of loss, which was impossible as long as all events and times were signs pointing to an eternal God, arises to block the reading process. Time, which was previously the medium in which God's plan unfolded, becomes equated with change (in whatever sense one understands that term), and meaning becomes problematic. Petrarch was very precise in calling his own era the "Dark Ages." Cut off by time from the Roman paradigm, one could not (within Petrarch's historical schema) know oneself or grasp the significance of contemporary events. In terms of his restructuring of history, medieval man is in very much the same situation as the pre-Christian pagan was in terms of salvation history. In both cases the gap between signs, linguistic or otherwise, and their ultimate referent is unbridgeable.

The poet of the *Canzoniere* does, in fact, identify his situation with that of Dante's virtuous heathen, who dwell in their own hemisphere of light, but are cut off from divine illumination. In *Canzone* 73 the speaker says of himself, *e vivo del desir fuor di speranza* (and I live on desire outside of hope [73. 78]), echoing Vergil's description of his own and his companions' fate in the first circle of *Inferno: . . . sanza speme vivemo in disio* (without hope we live in desire [*Inf.* IV, 42]). An earlier poem, Sonnet 16, however, qualifies this analogy, preventing us from taking the Dantesque framework which allows the comparison as our final frame of reference—preventing us, that is, from reducing Petrarch's poetics to a merely secular or idolatrous mode. This sonnet aggressively raises the fundamental issues of how, rather than what, its own signifiers signify, and how, differently from Dante's, they might be read:

Movesi il vecchierel canuto et bianco
del dolce loco ov' à sua età fornita
et da la famiglioula sbigottita
che vede il caro padre venir manco;
indi trahendo poi l'antiquo fianco
per l'extreme giornate di sua vita,
quanto piú pò, col buon voler s'aita,
rotto dagli anni, et dal camino stanco;

et viene a Roma, seguendo 'l desio,
per mirar la sembianza di colui
ch'ancor lassú nel ciel vedere spera:

così, lasso, talor vo cerchand'io,
donna, quanto è possibile, in altrui
la disïata vostra forma vera.

The white-haired old man leaves the sweet place where he has spent his life and the dismayed family which sees its dear father depart. Then dragging his old flanks through the last days of his life, as well as he can, he helps himself with his good will, broken by the years, and weary of the road. And he comes to Rome, following his desire, to gaze upon the likeness

of Him Whom he hopes to see again in heaven. Thus,
alas, sometimes I go searching, Lady, as much as it is
possible, in others for your desired true form.

For many readers, including the nineteenth-century Italian poet
Ugo Foscolo, the comparison between the devotion of a pilgrim
gazing at the image of his saviour and the poet's search for
images of his lady borders on blasphemy.[37] Wherever Petrarch
shocks, though, it is always to some end. The simile which
makes up most of this poem alludes as well to Dante the pilgrim, who, gazing in wonder at Saint Bernard in Canto XXXI of
Paradiso, also compares himself to a pilgrim beholding the
Veronica:

> *Qual è colui che forse di Croazia*
>   *viene a veder la Veronica nostra,*
>   *che per l'antica fame non sen sazia,*
> *ma dice nel pensier, fin che si mostra:*
>   *"Signor mio Iesù Cristo, Dio verace,*
>   *or fu sì fatta la sembianza vostra?";*
> *tal era io mirando la vivace*
>   *carità di colui che 'n questo mondo,*
>   *contemplando, gustò di quella pace.*

As is he who comes, perchance from Croatia to look on
our Veronica, and whose old hunger is not sated,
but says in thought, so long as it is
shown: "My Lord Jesus Christ, true God, was
then your semblance like to this?", such was I, gazing
on the living charity of him who, in this world, in
contemplation tasted of that peace. (*Par.* XXXI, 103–11)

This passage surprises because it seems to equate an unmediated
vision with the reading of an image (*la sembianza*) or sign.
The reverse situation, that of reading a sign as if it were that
which it represents, of mistaking the letter for the spirit, is
much more familiar in the *Commedia.* Dante's poem frequently
invokes the Pauline principle that, interpreted correctly, the material signs of this world reflect the truth which will be perceived directly in the Kingdom of God. The pilgrim's reaction
to his face-to-face encounter with Saint Bernard, as well as his
earlier "error" of taking the faces in the moon for mirror im-

ages (*Par.* III, 10–24), first of all allow us to savor vicariously the shock of unmediated vision. Dante discovers that his interpretive, or, in visual terms, perceptual habits paradoxically make reality as difficult for him to "see" face-to-face as it was in reflection. But his similes also draw our attention to the nature and status of this poetic effect. *We* are not in heaven; we have only the written transcription of that event, and, like the Croatian pilgrim looking upon the Veronica, we must keep questioning the relationship between this *sembianza* and what it reflects. As Dante becomes an anti-Narcissus, the reader has fewer and fewer means of avoiding Narcissus' fatal error, not knowing or having seen the reality of which the poem is the reflection, and therefore imagining their representational relationship, if at all, only with the greatest difficulty. As sign and referent become one for Dante the pilgrim, the gap separating them becomes a chasm for Dante the poet. The "true icon," a two-dimensional *sembianza* which may be seen only when its keepers deign to exhibit it, stands in a most tenuous relation to the Son of God. The figure of Saint Bernard, *che 'n questo mondo, / contemplando, gustò di quella pace,* recalls Dante's warning near the beginning of the *Paradiso* that only those who have already reached out for this nourishment, *Voialtri pochi che drizzaste il collo / per tempo al pan del li angeli* (You other few who lifted up your necks betimes for bread of angels [*Par.* II, 10–11]), will be able to follow him into these deep waters without losing their way.

It is a short step but a radical shift of emphasis from the dazzling metapoetics of *Paradiso* to the estrangement of letter from spirit to be inferred from Petrarch's sonnet. The Veronica simile reappears here, not as a figure for the face-to-face vision of the meaning hidden behind the veil, but for the way in which "meaning" inheres in the veil itself. Significantly, Petrarch's old man does not ask whether or not Christ looked like this image, and grammatically there is no direct connection between the two. Where they are linked correlatively, *or fu sì fatta la sembianza vostra,* in Dante's text, in Petrarch's they are doubly insulated from each other, the pronoun inferentially referring to Christ having been banished to a relative clause within a prepositional phrase: di *colui / ch'ancor lassú nel ciel vedere spera.* These grammatical and semantic differences correspond to an important distinction between the interpretive approaches of the two pilgrims. Dante's Croatian pilgrim anticipates (as Dante insists the reader of *Paradiso* must anticipate) a mutual dependence between sign and object. The image is a way of knowing Christ insofar as Christ is the way of understanding the image. For Petrarch's old man, on the other hand, this convenient circularity is broken. There is no indication or expectation that the image functions as a way of knowing Christ. On the contrary, Christ is altogether absent from the sonnet, and only the object pronoun of the prepositional phrase serves to identify the image whose own name (the Veronica or "true icon") is just as absent as that of Christ. It is solely the old man's desire, the poem implies, that allows him to see a *sembianza* at all in this image. The concluding tercet, presumably the tenor of the extended simile, both makes explicit the idolatrous aspect of such an approach to images, and distinguishes this relationship from idolatry in the Augustinian or Dantesque sense. The modifiers, *disiata, vostra,* and *vera,* all pile up around the term *forma* which, in turn, comes into existence somewhere between the questing lover and certain beings about whom all we know is that they are other, *altrui,* than the beloved. The lover looks for the "true form" of his beloved in others instead of looking directly for or at her because, imperfect as it is (*quanto è possibile*), this alienated *forma* is the only means available for apprehending "her." If the simile holds, then Laura herself is as inaccessible to the lover as Christ in heaven is to the still earth-bound old man. And as the equation of her with the heavenly Christ further indicates, this inaccessibility is not to be taken as the capricious behavior of a human being, but as an incontrovertible fact of life. The burden of the analogy is not that Laura deserves to be worshipped as much as Christ, but that the lover and the old man confront the same obstacles in pursuing their respective desires.

The entire octave of the sonnet is taken up with a description of the old man's leave-taking and of the hardship he suffers along the way he has chosen. (We never, in fact, hear of his reaching his goal, nor do we hear the outcome of the lover's quest for the true form of his beloved.) What this larger part of the poem has to do with the lover's situation is never made explicit, but there is no reason not to assume that they are related, that the lover, too, is traveling far from the comforts and familiarity of his society or tradition. If he is not physically old and weak, he nevertheless has reason to see himself, or his discourse, as "limping." More specifically, the old man who limps to Rome recalls Dante's representation of a pre-conversion "old" self trying to limp up the mountain of Purgatory before starting upon what for him is the right road. In Petrarch's sonnet the ways of error and of righteousness have apparently become indistinguishable. (Rome and Christ, it should be noted, seem not to be in conflict here.) If the sonnet may be read as a brief allegory of literary history, it shows the poet parting company with both past and present custom, but hardly in a position to claim that his new departure represents a "truer" way than that of his predecessors.

II
The Poetics
of the
Canzoniere

The story won't *tell* . . .
not in any literal,
vulgar way.

Henry James,
"The Turn of the Screw"

In the previous chapter we saw that, practically speaking, reading Petrarch's poetry involved reading Dante's as well, that significant dimensions of individual poems, as well as a more general sense of Petrarch's project, were illuminated by close comparisons between the two. In this chapter, I will argue that such comparison is, to a large extent, constitutive of the "meaning" of the *Canzoniere,* that one poet's poems do not, in this case, constitute themselves as an object of study until and unless they are read in comparison with poems by other poets. Because Petrarch's poetry in the *Canzoniere* orients itself particularly toward the *Commedia,* and because its poetics of indeterminacy redirects attention away from the poetic "subject" toward poetic relationships, I will discuss its points of significant difference from Dante's poem fairly extensively. Once the story of this relationship is unfolded, and we infer from it that the task of relational reading extends itself to poetic tradition or literary history more generally, the contrast I am attempting to describe between the poetics of Dante and Petrarch will have further relevance. Thus, Dante's poetics, as well as Petrarch's, becomes my subject, and it has seemed to me strategic to begin there.

Stylistic Motivation and Significance

In Canto XVII of *Paradiso,* Dante's ancestor Cacciaguida charges him to tell plainly and directly what he has seen on his journey. Setting the example himself with his homely metaphor of scratching where it itches, Cacciaguida warns that, though such candor might first offend, it is not only possible but imperative that Dante "set aside every falsehood" and "make manifest his vision":

> *Coscienza fusca*
> *o de la propria o de l'altrui vergogna*
> *pur sentirà la tua parola brusca.*
> *Ma nondimen, rimossa ogni menzogna,*
> *tutta tua vision fa manifesta;*
> *e lascia pur grattar dov' è la rogna.*

A conscience dark, either with its own or with another's shame, will indeed feel your speech to be harsh. But none the less, all falsehood set aside, make manifest all that you have seen; and then let them scratch where the itch is.[1] (*Par.* XVII, 124–29)

One question raised and to some extent answered by this formulation is that concerning the terms in which the vision might be made manifest. Dante's violation of surface decorum with the harsh line *e lascia pur grattar dov' è la rogna* functions as a stylistic exemplification of the candor Cacciaguida encourages, and calls attention to an important principle of the poetics of the *Commedia:* that the poem is a heterogeneous text, but one whose various strategies operate as if governed, not by the desires of fallen man or the conventions of his language, but by some principle of divine truth which lies on the other side of human discourse. In Charles S. Singleton's classic formulation, the *Commedia* is an "allegory" of a particular kind: ". . . not an allegory of 'this for that,' but an allegory of 'this *and* that,' of this sense plus that sense. . . . The words have a real meaning in pointing to a real event; the event, in its turn, has meaning because events wrought by God are themselves as words yielding a meaning, a higher and spiritual sense."[2] This may be overstating the case as proposed by Cacciaguida, who puts it that the discourse of the poem may at least be "not a lie," but the point Singleton so importantly grasps is that Dante's words can be double in significance without being ambiguous, not at least in our modern sense of doubtful or uncertain. Rather, double or multiple significances arrange themselves hierarchically, and this hierarchy, in turn, linguistically suggests confidence in an order or an ordering principle which is somehow immanent in the medium as well as beyond or outside of it. The corollary to Singleton's proposition, that the language of the *Commedia* operates as if God ultimately supports it, would be that the poem, in turn, seems to give access to that authority. Cacciaguida's bluntness indicates or enacts a certain faith that language can show forth or make manifest that on which it is based.

This passage in *Paradiso* benefits from Dante's having raised and continuing to raise linguistic issues of great complexity. Here the text's claim to "make manifest" is immediately made good but in a way which subsumes confidence in language's referentiality into a more complicated suggestion about how the capacity of language is, ultimately at least, guaranteed by God. Cacciaguida's charge continues:

> *Ché se la voce tua sarà molesta*
> *nel primo gusto, vital nodrimento*
> *lascerà poi, quando sarà digesta.*

> For if at first taste your voice be grievous,
> yet shall it leave thereafter vital nourishment
> when digested. (*Par.* XVII, 130–32)

Buried in this apparently figurative description of the responsibility borne by the reader of the poem to make good its "vision," there is an allusion which is virtually a quotation from Scripture. What appears at first to be a metaphorical elaboration, a movement away from plain speaking, actually draws us further inward toward the center of the poem's "meaning." The reference is to Revelations 10:9 where John is given a scroll by an angel who says, "Take the book and eat it, and it will be bitter to your stomach, but in your mouth it will be sweet as honey."[3] Dante has altered God's word to the extent necessary to take account of the different contexts in which it is heard. For John, eating the scroll in heaven, it is sweet to the taste, but becomes harsh as it is translated into a prophecy of earthly destruction. For Dante's readers the process is reversed; the seemingly harsh verdict of divine justice on the world which the *Commedia* relays would lead the poem's responsible readers to the nourishment of a higher truth. This reverse quotation of Scripture clearly complicates the notion of telling things as they are, raising questions of context, speaker, and audience, and thereby of the possibility, suggested by Singleton, that there is a stable relationship between linguistic signifiers and historical signifieds. These complications and questions, which must be taken into account before Cacciaguida's injunction can be obeyed, are partially dealt with in the next interpretive step that the Biblical allusion in this passage suggests.

The verse from Revelations is itself a near quotation, recalling the scene of prophetic election in Ezekiel 3:2: "Son of man, your stomach devour and your bowels be filled with this volume that I give to you. And I devoured it, and it was in my mouth as sweet as honey."[4] It is the word of God, rendered by Ezekiel in direct discourse, of which Dante ultimately catches a faint echo.[5] The effect of his quotation of a quotation of a quotation—complicated by the implicit lining up of Dante's readers with the prophets John and Ezekiel, of his vision to the divine "volume"—is to carry us back not only from text to text but also from context to context, seemingly in the direction of divine origin. Like several other gestures in the *Commedia,* most notably the pageant of Revelation in *Purgatorio* XXXIII where Dante and Statius join the procession of Old and New Testament authors, this repetition and variation of a Scriptural pattern indicate a typological continuity between poem and Scripture, reader and poem, the same kind of continuity as that between the Old and New Testaments. Thus, if Scripture, whatever its metaphorical and symbolic structures, finally stands in a quotational relationship to God (as the verse from Ezekiel seems to imply), then Dante's poem, though demonstrably referential only with respect to another text or texts, should be able to make a similar claim. Finally, as we shall see, the poem equivocates. In the words of one recent commentator, it "is continuously caught between the elusive claim of speaking with prophetic self-assurance and the awareness that this can be a supreme transgression."[6] But for the time being it is enough to note that, whether or not this claim is made good, Dante writes *as if* his text were prophetic.

Dante's invention of an entirely new verse form, *terza*

rima, is a case in point. Its newness corresponds to the newness of the prophecy it embodies. Its complex play on units of three calls attention, audaciously it might seem, to the omnipresence of the trinitarian principle throughout the temporal and metaphorical structures of the poem. When at times the *Commedia* is also made up of a tissue of the voices of previous poets—Pier delle Vigne in the canto of the suicides and Bertran de Born in the canto of the sowers of discord are typical examples, as are Vergil, Ovid, Statius, the *stilnovisti,* and others whose poetry is evoked more pervasively—the verse form, which quite literally harmonizes them with each other, would further suggest an ultimate compatibility for all the varied styles of "secular" literature. One purpose of bringing together tremendously varied styles by means of the new dispensation of *terza rima* would seem to be to show that the truth to which this poem would point is available everywhere, to all people, if only they know how to "digest" it, and that this poem is capable of teaching them to do so.

The considerations of Dante's stylistic motivation, of what and how stylistic features come to mean in the *Commedia,* suggest the basis for a similar investigation of stylistic and related formal features in the *Canzoniere.* Especially after Cacciaguida's injunction, from which we may infer that, for Dante, formal and stylistic gestures should not be understood by the poet or the reader as if they made no reference to ideological context and historical situation—that they become unintelligible when read, or rather unread, as if they existed autonomously—the question of how Petrarch formally and stylistically presents his text becomes central to an understanding of his poetic difference from Dante.

When we turn to the collection of three hundred and sixty-six poems by Petrarch which he entitled *Rerum vulgarium fragmenta* but which have come to be known as the *Canzoniere* or *Rime,* what is immediately striking is their stylistic sameness. Nowhere, certainly, do we find a drop in tone comparable to that of Cacciaguida. On the occasion of the sesquicentennial of Petrarch's death in 1974, one frustrated Italian journalist described the *Canzoniere* as having a lexicon "among the most monotonous in all of literature" and added that they were written in a style "whose movements at times require the sensitivity of a seismograph to detect."[7] Petrarch's habits of composition, about which we know something from the Latin memoranda in his manuscripts, suggest that the lexical and stylistic restrictedness of the collection, though not necessarily monotonous, was certainly deliberate. He could reorder and interpolate poems, apparently for purely formal reasons, and he tested individual compositions for unwanted dissonances by singing them aloud.[8] We are also likely to notice the contrast to the *Commedia* presented by Petrarch's adherence in the *Canzoniere* to traditional patterns of versification. His localized innovations are extraordinary, but they are established within the bounds of the lyric verse forms (the sonnet, the *canzone,* the *ballata,* the *madrigale,* and the *sestina*) developed by earlier Provençal and Italian vernacular poets. Both stylistically and technically, then, the poetry of the *Canzoniere* presents a tightly circumscribed field which contrasts sharply with the stylistically wide-ranging openness of Dante's poem.

These technical and stylistic dissimilarities between the *Commedia* and the *Canzoniere* might be attributable to nothing more than temperamental differences between the two poets, as in fact they often have been, were it not for a strange discrepancy between what Petrarch says he is doing and what, as far as we can tell, he actually is doing. In the opening sonnet, the poems of the *Canzoniere* are characterized as *rime sparse,* scattered rhymes, written in a *vario stile,* a varied style.[9] If we take the poet at his word, we must be puzzled when he offers us instead the limited repertory of established lyric verse forms. In Sonnet 40, similarly, he poses as the weaver of a new fabric, *la tela novella* (40. 2), within which, if certain conditions are met, he will weave together disparate truths, *l'un coll'altro vero accoppio* (40. 4). This sounds much more like what Dante is doing with *terza rima* than like anything we can find in the conventional verse forms and specialized vocabulary of the *Canzoniere.* These thematic comments, I would suggest, bear witness to a relationship between the two texts, underlying their dissimilarities. Though the apparent inconsistencies and crossed purposes within the *Canzoniere,* of which the above are just a small sample, have usually led readers to frustration with Petrarch and nostalgia for the wonderful lucidity of Dante, a comparison could be made which would account for many of the more puzzling features of the *Canzoniere*. Such a comparison seems to be openly invited by the sequence, but it cannot take place within an argument that makes Dante the standard against which to measure Petrarch's inability to tell a straight story or live up to his promises. Various descriptions, differently conceived, of intertextuality in general and this relationship in particular suggest, on the other hand, why this question should be posed and how it might be framed.

One Dantist who appreciates the differences between the two poets without prejudice to either one has usefully suggested that "the contrast between Dante's epic ruggedness and Petrarch's lyrical smoothness . . . implies a radically divergent theory of language."[10] The trouble with this formulation is that, on the one hand, it drives the two poets apart into possibly incommensurable poetic fields, and, on the other hand, it assumes that Petrarch has available to him a "theory" of the same order as, even if different from, Dante's. Importantly, though, it admits the possibility that stylistic attributes of Petrarch's poetry, like smoothness, might imply something specific about the nature of that poetry. In his recent studies of poetic influence Harold Bloom suggests why comparison is part of the intrinsic meaning of any poem. He argues that a poem does not exist as a self-sufficient entity but as a strategy for meeting a situation left by precursors, and that only in such a situation can poetic identity be forged. The chief consequences of this theory for practical criticism are a redefinition of the object of study— "there are no texts, but only relationships between texts"—and a concomitant methodological shift of focus—"to interpret a poem, necessarily you interpret its differences from other poems."[11] Bloom's theory is especially helpful in reading a poet like Petrarch whose reputation as the precursor or point of origin of modern poetry often leads commentators to mystify not only the lyrics themselves, but also the significance of a literary "crossing" which is often spoken of as completely disjunctive.[12]

The relational impulse of the reading process recommended by Bloom would be short-circuited, however, if broadly based conceptual and cultural difference and change were ignored. If the assumption of the autonomy of the individual poem were simply replaced with an assumption that poetic history is autonomous (and always consistent for the literary history), then the results of the comparison would become a foregone conclusion. One would always find a poetic son locked in battle with a poetic father. The possibility that the Freudian "father" on whom Bloom's "precursor poet" is modeled might also tend to become hypostatized in a discussion of poetic influence presents a further problem, but suggests a way of thinking that circumvents the former interpretive cul-de-sac. The "father" in Freud could be considered not only a biological entity, but also the representative within the family structure of the whole sociological and political matrix in terms of which the child will have to re-define him- or herself in order to move from the position of child to the position of adult.[13] In other words, whatever matrix defines the individual as a child must be challenged and in some way revised in order that the same individual may become a full-fledged member of, rather than a dependent on, adult society, and the struggle with the father is one way in one culture of symbolically enacting this challenge. Similarly, the poet may be said to struggle with previous poets as a way of testing and revising a whole set of signifying possibilities of which s/he wishes to become a user and shaper. Put another way, the poet must work within the language s/he inherits if s/he is to say anything at all, while, in order to speak the "truth," in order not to remain a child or prisoner of language, s/he has to posit him- or herself as a more or less radical antagonist of this structure.

By replacing the notion of personal combat with a model of system transition as a whole, we alter the scope and purpose of relational reading.[14] The method itself is freed of a priori typologies for the interpretation of individual texts and intertextual relationships. This revision also shows literature to be subject to influences that are not solely personal or formal. Because the circumstances of the writer embrace the whole symbolic system into which s/he has been born, literary systems can be limited and changed under pressure from conditions and shifts in other areas of symbolic action. Literary interpretation can become one way of apprehending those conditions and shifts, while the theoretical presumption that such changes have occurred and may continue to occur (a theoretical position which involves itself in its own problematic of contingency) necessarily influences how and what the interpreter interprets. Most important for my purposes, we now have a way of distinguishing literary and/or historical "crisis" from the gradual evolution of symbolic systems that the use of Bloom's theory might appear to universalize.[15]

The intellectual historian Hayden White characterizes the kind of crisis that I think the relationship between Dante and Petrarch puts before us in terms of just such a distinction:

> Periods of genuine "crisis" in literary history . . . must be seen as those in which new systems of encodation and transmission of messages are being constituted, as times when language itself has fallen under question, and none of the conventional modes of message formulation and transmission appear to be adequate for naming and classifying the elements of the larger historical-natural context. In such times it is not so much the principles of selection that come under scrutiny as the principles of combination themselves. . . .[16]

The distinction between questioning principles of selection and questioning principles of combination is especially useful in a comparative reading of two poets like Dante and Petrarch, whose differences of concern were argued in chapter one to be finally minimal, but whose difference of mode is conspicuously great. It is also important to stress that the constitution of "new systems of encodation and transmission" and the scrutiny of "conventional modes of message formulation" are different names for the same gesture. White, I think, aptly captures the ambivalence of a writer in this position. My only reservation about this formulation is that it threatens to reintroduce the split between literature and history (opposing them as entity to context). Assuming that poets locate themselves with respect to other poets *as a way of locating themselves in their own time and place,* this separation is unnecessary.

Returning, now, to the question of the stylistic differences between Dante's *Commedia* and the *Canzoniere* with the expectation of finding them in some way symptomatic of historical "crisis" or change, we discover that the formal restrictedness of the latter text takes on a special significance which illuminates Petrarch's paradoxical reference to the *rime sparse* and the *vario stile*. In the *Commedia* the allusive range, the innovative verse form, and the stylistic texture of the poem represented the intention of an allegorical adequation of linguistic signifier to historical signified. The texture of Petrarch's lyrics, comparatively consistent from poem to poem, is, on the other hand, conspicuously distanced from the emotional turmoil and spiritual conflict presented thematically. Similarly, Petrarch's commitment to verse forms invented by others makes us wary of trying to bridge that gap even when formal structures exquisitely diagram the weariness or confusion the poet claims as his own. With this interpretive expectation, it appears that where Dante's poem stylistically indicated the hermeneutic relationship between its poetics and the truth to be attained through the poem, Petrarch's poetry signals a severing of that connection—a "crisis"—or at least a shift—a "change" in the locus of error. Where for Dante error would be more a matter of the reader than of the text, for Petrarch error and its concomitant problems for reading and readability become located in the text itself.

What the opening sonnet says serves as a warning and should be taken literally: the persona or "self" apparently constituted by the sequence could be, whatever else it might also be, an illusion suggested by the physical contiguity and the superficial resemblance of these poems to one another.[17] The lines in which the term *rime sparse* is embedded enact a disconnectedness between the poems and the poet that sets the poems adrift from whatever stability even an historical "self" has to offer:

> *Voi ch'ascoltate in rime sparse il suono*
> *di quei sospiri ond'io nudriva'l core . . .*

> You who hear in scattered rhymes the sound of
> those sighs with which I nourished my heart. . .
> (1. 1–2).

As a recent reader has pointed out, what the audience of Petrarch's poetry is to hear "is not the direct utterance of the *sospiri*, Petrarch's sighs, but rather their sound, their *suono*. The *suono* is in turn that of verses."[18] The same reader finds that in the second stanza "there is a deliberate ambiguity in the syntax of this expression of his hope":

del vario stile in ch'io piango e ragiono
fra le vane speranze e'l van dolore,
ove sia chi per prova intenda amore,
spero trovar pietà, non che perdono.

for the varied style in which I weep and speak
between vain hopes and vain sorrow, where there
is anyone who understands love through experience,
I hope to find pity, not only pardon. (1. 5–8).

It could be that he hopes *his suffering* will produce the antici-pated effect in the reader, or it could be that he hopes something about *the poetry itself* will evoke the reader's *pietà*.[19] I would go even farther and say that the ambiguity extends to the term *vario stile.* Conventionally the term would refer to variations intrinsic to the language of the *Canzoniere.* Then Petrarch could be saying that, as in the *Commedia,* stylistic variation is an effort to approximate varieties of experience. But Petrarch's *vario stile* could include the notion that style (and/or his *stilus* or pen) operates independently of, at variance from, experi-ence. Since Petrarch's stylistic range is, in fact, highly restricted, and since the whole poem is very hedgy about the relationship between language and experience, the second interpretation seems equally appropriate. Why, then, does Petrarch risk being misunderstood by referring to his poetry as if it were like Dante's? We might conjecture that, just as the term *vario stile* can be read both ways, so a poetic *stile* can be accepted as no less adequate than Dante's to the complexities of the relation-ship between language and experience, while it can also be taken to display a significantly different understanding from Dante's of that relationship. The task of reading the *Canzoniere* would then become, largely, one of delineating that difference within the context of inter-reference.

It is specifically within the range of willfully deceptive discourse, associated by Dante with the sinners of *Inferno,* that the *Canzoniere* often implicitly locates itself and its language. What this might indicate becomes apparent only gradually, over the course of the entire sequence, but the fact that this will be one of its major motifs is already stated in the opening sonnet:

> *et del mio vaneggiar vergogna è 'l frutto,*
> *e 'l pentersi, e 'l conoscer chiaramente*
> *che quanto piace al mondo è breve sogno.*

> and of my raving, shame is the fruit, and
> repentance, and the clear knowledge that what
> ever pleases in the world is a brief dream. (1. 12–14)

These lines fall into two parts, the first of which names the *Canzoniere*'s ostensibly "wild" mode of discourse (*mio vaneggiar*), the second of which says what this mode of discourse is good for (*'l conoscer chiaramente*). They are paradoxical only in terms of an expectation that knowledge corresponds to truth. In the absence of any such expectation the lines seem to say, straightforwardly enough, that any sense of position and of self afforded by this language is illusory—but illusory in a particular way. The *frutto* of *vaneggiar* is not an epistemology implying a positive ontology (considered as such it becomes a bitter fruit of *vergogna* and *'l pentersi,* an awareness of lack and loss, for Petrarch's persona), but Petrarch's *vaneggiar* nevertheless can bear the vigorous fruit of an understanding, a "clear knowledge," of the mechanism of its own epistemological dream. If it is also the case, as I believe it is, that this poem alludes to *Paradiso* XVII, then the poet here is assuming the role of Cacciaguida vis-à-vis the reader, promising a "fruitfulness" which could be interpreted as both (either) bitter and (or) sweet.[20]

A look at three more poems will more fully explicate Petrarch's appeal to Infernal discourse and his understanding, different from Dante's, of how such discourse operates. In *Canzone* 73 where, as I mentioned in the previous chapter, the poet's situation is identified with that of Dante's Vergil and the other virtuous heathen, the speaker goes on to say that were he not "tongue-tied," he would write in a "new" way:

> *et vivo del desir fuor di speranza:*
> *solamente quel nodo*
> *ch'amor cerconda a la mia lingua quando*
> *l'umana vista il troppo lume avanza,*

*fosse disciolto, i' prenderei baldanza
di dir parole in quel punto sì nove
che farian lagrimar chi le 'ntendesse.*

and I live on desire outside of hope: if only
that knot which love ties around my tongue when
the excess of light overpowers my mortal sight were
loosened, I would take boldness to speak words at
that moment so new that they would make all who
heard them weep. (translation mine) (73. 79–84)

Petrarch's term *novo* carries a technical sense here. The barely submerged reference of *parole . . . nove* to the end of the *Vita Nuova,* where Dante vows to write about Beatrice that which has never been written of any other woman,[21] identifies the poetics of the *Canzoniere,* at least up to this point, as "not new" in the moral and epistemological sense claimed for itself by the *Commedia.* By implication, Petrarch's language is "old," comparable to the language of the pre-conversion "old man" in the younger Dante whose will (and whose language) has not yet been made *libero, dritto, e sano* (*Purg.* XXVII, 140). A further allusion, the *nodo,* which is Dante's term for any impediment to the intellect or will in the journey to Paradise, seems again to identify the poet's language as "old" in an absolute moral and epistemological sense. But Petrarch's conflation in this passage of the words of the younger Dante who goes on to write *Paradiso* and those of Dante's Vergil who has no hope of Paradise suggests that the poetic problem to be confronted by Petrarch does not concern the will, but indeed *solamente quel nodo,* which is appropriately given prominence in a line of its own. The allusion to Dante's Vergil, which suggests that no alteration in moral stance is to be expected, can be reconciled with the evocation of the younger Dante, ready to take on whatever is poetically necessary in order to write about his desire, only if the knot appears to Petrarch to be of an entirely linguistic nature and hence not subject to "will." Whether or not it may be untied, this *nodo* could then justifiably be taken by the poet as the subject of his own poetry of desire, as in fact it already has been and will continue to be, without the poet having to fear that his words will be understood by himself or by his readers simply as signs of personal transgression. (If he is correct, that the problem lies in language, then it would, of course, be mistaken to read for patterns of sinfulness or virtue.) The paradox pointed to by the double allusion to Dante's Vergil and to Dante the prophetic poet is that Petrarch's good faith, however spiritually akin to Dante's, must be indicated precisely by not writing in Dante's "new" (though chronologically older) way.

Two sonnets, which are widely separated in the text, but which treat similar concerns, explain thematically how the diversion of attention away from questions of morality or will toward purely linguistic problems is becoming inevitable, why Infernal discourse in particular needs to be understood not as a function of willful perversion but as the appropriate subject and discourse of poetry. The poet, it appears in Sonnet 49, has tried to follow Cacciaguida's advice to Dante (at least the injunction to remove every lie from his discourse), but to no avail. He complains that although he guards his tongue against falsehood, it seems simply to malfunction as a consequence:

> Perch'io t'abbia guardato di menzogna
> a mio podere et onorato assai,
> ingrato lingua, già però non m'ai
> renduto honor, ma facto ira e vergogna;
> ché quando più 'l tuo aiuto mi bisogna
> per dimandar mercede, allor ti stai
> sempre più fredda, et se parole fai,
> son imperfecte, et quasi d'uom che sogna.

> Although I have kept you from lying, as far as I
> could, and paid you much honor, ungrateful tongue,
> still you have not brought me honor but shame and
> anger; for, the more I need your help to ask for
> mercy, the more you become always colder, and if
> you form any words they are broken and like those
> of a man dreaming. (translation mine) (49. 1–8)

Here the poet speaks as if he still aspired to a mode of discourse that would not be like dreaming. The characteristics of this discourse would include "wholeness" and "warmth," as opposed to the fragmentation and coldness of the discourse to which the poet finds himself condemned here. Significantly, this opposition is presented in physiological terms that link it to a distinction between speech and writing—a distinction which is implicit as well in the opposition between "old" and "new" words. Up to this point, the poet has been able only to "write," to form words whose only connection to each other and to individuals or events beyond themselves has remained an unrealized wish. "Speech," on the other hand, would be a language organically related to the speaker, unproblematically "whole" in itself and faithful to what it represents. The poet's desire to "speak," though, may also be seen as a function of his view of writing. As the poem already "knows," but the persona Petrarch adopts does not, the reason that the former seems to be a possibility, why anything other than "speech" appears to be an utter failure of language, lies in an oversight on the poet's part. In the sestet of the sonnet, he overlooks a subtle example of his own "writing" which he mistakes for "speech" or its equivalent. There, although his speech defect spreads to other modes of expression (tears and sighs), his assertion that his facial expression is "not silent" implies that his linguistic dysfunction can be, if not cured, at least compensated for:

> *Lagrime triste, et voi tutte le notti*
> *m'accompagnate, ov'io vorrei star solo,*
> *poi fuggite dinanzi a la mia pace;*
> *et voi sí pronti a darmi angoscia et duolo,*
> *sospiri, allor traete lenti et rotti:*
> *sola la vista mia del cor non tace.*

> Sad tears, you also every night accompany me,
> when I wish to be alone, and then you flee when
> my peace comes! And you, sighs, so ready to give me
> anguish and sorrow, then you move slow and broken.
> Only my eyes are not silent about my heart. (49. 9–14)

The gesture which connects *la vista* and *il cor* as signifier and signified is not taken by the poet here to be an operation of visual representation, such as writing is; it therefore mistakenly seems to him to escape the short-circuiting of words, tears, and sighs, and, paradoxically, to fulfill the dream of living speech. If he should catch himself in the act of first having to constitute the relationship that creates this illusion of continuity and wholeness of being, he would be in a position to recognize his words, tears, and sighs, as neither the failure nor the fulfillment of a language, neither necessarily cold and broken, nor possibly whole and warm, "redemptive" and "ennobling." The poet has discovered that all that appears to be writing is "imperfect and like that of a man who dreams." It remains for him to discover, and the Petrarchan text to display, that this operation of writing itself generates the sense of an alternative that would be vocal, organic, and ethically and spiritually rewarding.[22]

In Sonnet 170, after various ramifications of the fundamental problem of writing have been discovered and pondered in many of the intervening *rime,* the recognition process advances, even as the situation to be recognized is portrayed thematically to be more general and more hopeless than the poet first supposed. In other words, the lover comes closer than before to understanding that "writing" itself forms the imperfect, uncertain basis of his desire for wholeness and completeness. Here he realizes that the problematic of his language extends to that of others as well:

> *Ond' io non poté' mai formar parola*
> *ch'altro che da me stesso fosse intesa:*
> *così m'ha fatto Amor tremante et fioco.*
> *Et veggi' or ben che caritate accesa*
> *lega la lingua altrui, gli spirti invola:*
> *chi pò dir com'egli arde, è 'n picciol foco.*

> Whence I have never been able to form a word that was
> understood by any but myself, Love has made me
> so trembling and weak. And I now see well that
> kindled charity ties one's tongue [in general],
> steals away spirits: he who can say how
> he burns is in but a little fire. (translation
> mine) (170. 9–14)

Both these lines and the lines in *Inferno* XXVI that the phrase *gli spirti invola* alludes to require careful reading. Let us turn to Dante's critique of Ulysses' claims to full "speech" first.

In the canto of Ulysses, the fraudulent counselors appear as flames moving along the bottom of a ditch. The poem makes it clear that the pilgrim is strongly attracted to this scene. One of the flames in particular attracts the pilgrim's attention because it is cloven at the top. Dante comments to Vergil that it resembles the funeral pyre of Eteocles and his brother. (Eteocles is named; Polynices is not. We may recall that it was Eteocles who broke the agreement to share the rulership of Thebes, refusing to pass the throne on to his brother at the end of the stipulated year, thereby precipitating the war of the Seven against Thebes. Eteocles and Polynices were, of course, the heirs of their father-brother Oedipus whose own authority was, unbeknownst to himself, based upon the slaying of his father.) Vergil informs Dante that within the significantly-shaped flame two of the damned, Ulysses and Diomed, are tormented. Vergil asserts wrongly, however (at least in the case of Ulysses), that this punishment is for crimes of fraudulence committed during the Trojan War. In other words, Vergil, the "virtuous" guide, deceives and is self-deceived at the moment he confuses the version of Imperial Roman history which he himself wrote (and in which Ulysses is cast as an enemy of Rome) with providential history which, we subsequently infer, condemns Ulysses for a different reason—as it also condemned Vergil himself. When the greater of the two horns of flame (that which encases Ulysses, we now know) is urged to "speak," we are led to reflect on a pattern introduced in the preliminary description of these strange tongues, repeated in Vergil's error, and exemplified in the whole history of Thebes evoked by the pilgrim. As the flames move along the "throat" of the ditch, we are told, *nessuna mostra il furto, / e ogni fiamma un peccatore invola* (not one shows its theft, and each flame steals away a sinner [*Inf.* XXVI, 41–42]). That is, these flames which superficially resemble *la fiamma sola, / sì come nuvoletta* (the flame alone, like a little cloud [*Inf.* XXVI, 38–39]) of the prophet Elijah's chariot, perpetrate a deception because of their resemblance to an image of transcendence. Unlike an ordinary flame which we know to be the tangible manifestation of an invisible combustion process which in turn is based upon the material being consumed, these flames *appear* to stand free of any material basis, to be complete, clear, and significant in and of themselves. Only because we are told that this is *not* the case do they become significant in the more ordinary sense, signifying their material basis. Similarly our knowledge of Vergil's personal and na-

tional biases makes his mistaken characterization of Ulysses'
sins intelligible (the text of the canto does not finally contra-
dict, but "arranges" itself, according to this awareness). In a
darker sense, perhaps, the positions of authority assumed by
Oedipus and Eteocles become intelligible once it is known that
the former has killed his father and the latter denies his
brother.

In all three cases, the assumed position of authority could
be shown to be based upon a prior situation which has merely
been effaced or denied in the assumption of that authority—an
"authority" which would then appear highly contingent rather
than absolute. Ulysses' reported oration to his followers re-
enacts the "Oedipal" strategy as it is involved in what Petrarch
would call "speech," and it becomes incumbent upon us to
discover the denial, effacement, or deception it performs:

> "O frati," dissi, "che per cento milia
>   perigli siete giunti a l'occidente,
>   a questa tanto picciola vigilia
> d'i nostri sensi ch'è del rimanente
>   non vogliate negar l'esperienza,
>   di retro al sol, del mondo sanza gente.
> Considerate la vostra semenza:
>   fatti non foste a viver come bruti,
>   ma per seguir virtute e canoscenza."

> "O brothers," I said, "who through a hundred
> thousand dangers have reached the west, to
> this so brief vigil of our senses that remains
> to us, choose not to deny experience, following
> the sun, of the world that has no people.
> Consider your origin: you were not made to
> live as brutes, but to pursue virtue and
> knowledge." (Inf. XXVI, 112–20)

This passage supports a richer reading than I can give here,[23]
but one of its most striking ironies is Ulysses' encouragement
of his men to fulfill their epic identities in "the unpeopled
world." An epic hero is constituted as such only by the national
cause in terms of which his actions are deemed heroic, as
Vergil's misrepresentation of Ulysses the *Greek* hero serves to

remind us. Similarly, Ulysses fails to point out the social and historical nature of the "virtue," "knowledge," and "experience" he can here use as incentives only by taking them to be more basic than the human contexts in terms of which they make sense. He abuses the power of language to be abstract— to structure or govern contingency retrospectively—by "forgetting" or "stealing away" the whole complex of relationships that generates and supports these abstractions (Ulysses specifically leaves his *family* behind). This sleight of hand amounts to a reification of the process of linguistic representation (the "flame" of language should always be understood to be in process, never objectified, Dante's ingenious image implies); and the reified image is taken (wrongly, according to Dante) as itself the origin and hence the goal of human endeavor.

If Ulysses remains hidden from himself and his followers, though, he does not remain hidden from the pilgrim and the reader who have the means of "reading" the hidden motions of which his "speech" is merely a manifestation. In Petrarch's poem, on the other hand, where the lovers are stolen away in relative silence—*veggi' or ben che caritate accesa / lega la lingua altrui, gli spirti invola*—this reading process has become impossible. Their problem seems to be that although they are not literally at a loss for words, their words are not "language" in Dante's sense. They do not constitute even a deceptive image of hidden actions (*chi pò dir com' egli arde, è 'n picciol foco* [emphasis mine]). It is worth noting in this regard, that the term for desire in this poem is *caritate*, a term used only one other time in the sequence, in *Canzone* 28, to describe the high-mindedness and high accomplishment of Giovanni Colonna. Its use here is consistent with the idea that linguistic difficulties are no longer being attributed to the poet's own, possibly perverse, *desio*, but rather to words themselves (in this case, *caritate*— precisely the word which would attempt to name the true origin and goal of human endeavor) which here have no residue allowing for their allegorical construction or "allegorical" demystification. The crux of Sonnet 170 is the recognition that for language to reveal its own deception, or even for it to be deceptive in Dante's sense, it must point elsewhere than to itself; it must be "allegorical." If language is not allegorical, as Petrarch suggests that for him it is not, then Dante's metaphysics of desire breaks down because desire can *only* be identified or "known" in the mistaken, literal-minded way which seduces a Ulysses.

The first two stanzas of the sonnet indicate that *both* the poet's hope and his despair of ever fulfilling his desire are functions of his "readings" of the beloved's appearance:

> *Più volte già dal bel sembiante humano*
> *ò preso ardire co le mie fide scorte*
> *d'assalir con parole honeste accorte*
> *la mia nemica in atto humile et piano.*
> *Fanno poi gli occhi suoi mio penser vano*
> *perch'ogni mia fortuna, ogni mia sorte,*
> *mio ben, mio male, et mia vita, et mia morte,*
> *quei che solo il pò far, l'à posto in mano.*

> Many times already from the beautiful human
> semblance I have taken courage with my faithful
> escorts to assail with honest sagacious words my
> enemy, in bearing humble and soft. Her eyes
> then make my thought futile, because all my
> fortune, all my fate, my good, my evil, and
> my life and my death, he who alone can do so has
> put into her hand. (translation mine) (170. 1–8)

It is particularly significant that these lines do *not* say that the beloved changes her aspect or behavior. The reason her eyes make the poet's first thought futile is rather *his* realization, at the beginning of the second quatrain, that whatever positive significance the beloved appears to confer on his words is and has been a function of his own desire (of the "he" or Love which has placed all significance in the hands of the beloved). But if this positive significance may be seen as a function of the poet's own desire, the same must be said for the negative significance, the futility or vanity of his discourse, which her eyes are also said to occasion. Indeed, the same *is* said and said simultaneously: it is precisely "because" of the same desire that the poet's words now seem completely ineffectual, where many times (as he has just been saying) they seem or seemed potentially effective. In the sestet, where the beloved disappears altogether, the poet goes on to acknowledge that none of his words

(including, presumably, these that we are reading) has escaped
the circularity of these two (alternative?) "readings" of the
"writing" of his own desire—*Ond'io non potè mai formar
parola / ch'altro che da me stesso fosse intesa.* As was not yet
acknowledged, or only partially acknowledged in Sonnet 49, a
fundamental defect is intrinsic to the discourse of the desiring
self whose "position" in language is always already neither true
nor false but indeterminate. We are left with the amusing and
logical paradox that only a self whose desire is very slight (assuming this were possible) can say how he desires—*chi pò dir
com'egli arde, è in picciol foco*—which would be, of course, to
say very little if anything at all. The poet's alternatives prove to
be not writing vs. speech, but writing vs. not-writing.

Petrarch's characterization and justification of his mode of
writing in these (and many other) individual poems has far-
reaching implications for the *reading* of the *Canzoniere.* If we
have, in fact, taken Petrarch's writing as a record, even a fictive
record of historical experience, if we have been reading the sequence allegorically in Dante's complex sense of that term,
then it behooves us to reassess this understanding—a process
that we are encouraged to do at any and all points in the sequence, and one which the poet himself, as I shall explain
later, enacts as well. One significant discovery which is made
via this retrospective reading is not that significant symbolic
likenesses and relationships emerge from different dramatic
situations, but that with no apparent strain we have inferred
the same experience from metaphors diametrically opposed to
one another. In Sonnet 17 and again in *Canzone* 23 the poet
describes the freezing effect that the turning away of his beloved has upon him:

> *Ma gli spiriti miei s'aghiaccian poi
> ch'i' veggio, al departir, gli atti soavi
> torcer da me le mie fatali stelle.*

> but my spirits then turn cold, for I see at
> parting the gentle gestures twisting my fatal
> stars away from me. (translation mine) (17. 9–11)

Since twice before *sole* has been used as a synonym for Laura
(in Sonnets 4 and 9), the metaphor seems an apt expression

of the anguish occasioned by her departure. Later in *Canzone* 23, however, the poet compares what happens to him when his beloved leaves to the melting of snow in the sun. This is the difficult *canzone delle metamorfosi,* where, as he is about to describe his transformation into a fountain, the poet writes:

> *Ivi accusando il fugitivo raggio,*
> *a le lagrime triste allargai 'l freno*
> *et lasciaile cader come a lor parve;*
> *né già mai neve sotto al sol disparve*
> *com'io senti' me tutto venir meno.*

> There, blaming the fleeing ray, I loosed
> the rein to sad tears and let them fall
> as they willed; nor did ever snow under
> the sun disappear, as I felt myself
> entirely melt. (23. 112–16)

Once again we have no difficulty "understanding" this line, and oddly enough, it seems to confirm what we have learned before. But if we notice the imagistic instability, then we must ask ourselves where this sense of meaning is coming from, how it is constituted. Obviously syntax and context are important, but the operation of these particular images implies a more extreme position than that conventional grammar and word order are largely responsible for "meaning." The poet's sudden thaw, though indicative of no substantive change in his relationship to Laura, is nevertheless motivated. While lover and beloved are still estranged, the images of snow and sun have come together for the first time in the space of a single line, with the predictable result—a dissolution. By means of this language game Petrarch demonstrates precisely what he says in Sonnet 49, that though he does not lie, he cannot tell the truth. On the one hand, signs (like snow and sun) are operating according to some internal logic, but, on the other hand, the poet cannot stabilize this operation by guaranteeing that the relationships between sets of signs (Laura:sun :: poet:ice or snow) will remain constant. Although these signs are meaningful, this meaning cannot be conceived of as grounded either within or beyond the signifying system itself.

It gradually becomes apparent that the interpretive process

whereby we equate freezing and thawing with the same anguish is itself open to question. Specifically, this interpretation is a purely linguistic product occasioned by the repetition of that most unreliable of all linguistic elements, the shifter "I" whose relationship to itself, not to mention its relationship to the poet, has been in question since the opening sonnet. One consequence of *Canzone* 23, where the sun migrates from Laura to the poet and where the snow quite literally disappears, is to close off the possibility that the pronominal confusion with which the *Canzoniere* opens can be explained satisfactorily by the confused mental state of the poet. As the sequence has begun to show, it is the "I" itself, which, while it serves as the (pro)nominal center of Petrarch's linguistic universe, is also its most question-able element.

The play of the images "snow" and "sun" achieves a kind of ironic closure, when we realize that in *Sestina* 30 it is Laura who is associated with snow, while already in Sonnet 18 the poet has appropriated the properties of heat and light. With this chiastic exchange, the system of differences, which has al-ready become suspect, threatens to collapse into a series of iden-tities which makes our "understanding" of this web of signifi-cance even more problematic. We no longer have the means of keeping separate the two terms—poet/Laura or I/you—which seem to have been the occasion for this discourse. At the same time, though, our investigation of identity and difference points us in another direction, toward a somewhat different conception of the motivation of this literary production.

Returning to *Canzone* 23, we are told that difference is inevitably maintained *within* identity. In this retrospective re-capitulation of his career, the lover tells how love and the be-loved have driven him through a series of transformations—from man to laurel tree, to a swan, to a rock, to a fountain, to a piece of flint, to a man again, to a deer pursued by his hounds, and finally to an eagle bearing aloft his beloved in his words. In the end, however, he asserts that he has never left the laurel: *Ne per nova figura il primo alloro seppi lassar* (Nor for a new figure have I known how to leave the first laurel [23. 167]). Even if we took this line to mean simply that through all his variations of mood the poet has remained constant to his be-loved, homonymically referred to by the laurel, we would still have to deal with the ambiguity of the initial transformation whereby the man becomes the laurel and yet suffers because of his absence from it. But the terms *nova,* whose technical sense in the *Canzoniere* we have already noted, and *figura,* which is richly laden with connotations of classical and medieval theories of rhetoric and the interpretation of allegory,[24] give this line a metapoetic dimension which clarifies that problem. Read as a comment on how the poem works, this line says that no matter how novel or farfetched (*che udi mai d'uom nascer fonte?*), all of the transformations following the laurel point back to that laurel—none of them is "new." Entering into the figural process (the man becoming the laurel) allows for novel transformations or metaphorizations of the production of that "first figure," but these further transformations serve to figure only that figural production. That is, they represent not another (medieval, Dantesque) occasion for the figural *reading* of an allegorical narrative, but rather *the production in writing* of the figural structure itself. In having these further figures governed by the "first laurel," so that in them the poet cannot attain significant difference, Petrarch undercuts the authority of an allegorical narrative reading, demonstrating that the first figure itself is generated in an equally figural and arbitrary structural moment: the poet becoming identical with the laurel/Laura in one dimension (that of the linguistic signifier or figure), but remaining absent and different from it in another (that of the allegorical or interpretive reading, or figural significance).

Pursuing the inquiry into difference and identity we find, as often happens in the *Canzoniere,* that Petrarch's thematic indication in this poem is illustrated by a formal design in other poems. The poem just before this *canzone* as well as the thirtieth poem in the series are examples of the *sestina,* a verse form which occurs nine times in the *Canzoniere,* the ninth example being a *sestina doppia* which might appear to be one of Petrarch's few concessions to mimesis since it concerns the doubling of his grief upon Laura's death, but which is also a fabulous *tour de force* that intensifies the vertiginous construction and deconstruction of differences and identities. In the *sestina,* composed of six stanzas of six lines each, plus a three-line *congedo* or closing, each of the six words ending the six lines of the first stanza must be reused in a different order as line endings in each of the subsequent five stanzas, and all six words must be used once again, three of them as line endings, in the *congedo*. Leslie Fiedler has speculated on the significance of this form:

> . . . the resemblance-difference we have learned to expect from ordinary rhyming is separated out; the difference insisted upon from line to line; the resemblance become identity, suggested only from stanza to stanza. . . . In addition, the *sestina* is presided over by a kind of cold mathematics that functions like fate. In each of the six stanzas, the same six monorhymes must be repeated . . . until all the mathematical possibilities are exhausted. Then there is added a *commiato* or *congedo* in which the six key words must be crowded into only three lines. There is scant room left for invention; what free will is permitted must survive between closely restricted limits, until, at the conclusion, there is scarcely space for it to function at all.[25]

A similar operation brings sun and snow together in *Canzone* 23 and pressures images into the bewildering polyvocality which allows them to cross the boundaries they seem to set up. In fact, as I am not the first to argue, the form of the *sestina* provides a useful paradigm of the operation of the *Canzoniere* as a whole.[26] Fiedler's use of the loaded terms "cold mathematics" and "fate," however, obscures half of the story. It is true that the poet's freedom to write in a "new" way is restricted, but as we have seen, for Petrarch, this freedom is always illusory. Furthermore, the repetition of the same six line endings in all six possible arrangements implicitly challenges the assumption that these words and the syntax within which they are embedded were ever "about" anything but themselves. The line endings are quite literally re-presenting themselves. The freedom of this kind of poetry, on the other hand, lies in its emancipation from any allegorical residue. The process of systematic repetition, by undercutting the illusion of experiential reference, distances words from their conventional associations, leaving them "free" to interact with each other within the linguistic universe they constitute. Only when we have begun to see one impulse of this poetry as the emancipation of language from the interpretive habits of a discredited system of referentiality do its strange migrations and stubborn resistances begin to make a new kind of sense whose power has long been felt but whose uncompromising rigor has rarely been acknowledged.[27]

The net effect of combining and recombining words in this way, Adelia Noferi has maintained, is to make them other than themselves, to reinvent them. Petrarch, she says, arranges words in certain spatial relationships at certain distances from each other such that they reveal all their latent possibilities and acquire an aura of remote intensity.[28] Petrarch does speak of his love for Laura as that which rescues him from the common throng—*questa sola dal vulgo m'allontana* (72. 9). And certainly no one can read Sonnets 196, 197, and 198 beginning, respectively, *L'aura serena, L'aura celeste,* and *L'aura soave,* especially in the context of a series of poems about the poet's love for "Laura," and not feel that those syllables have been volatilized into something at once richer and airier than a simple breeze. But Noferi is more optimistic than the poet himself at times appears to be about the possibility of sustaining this effect which, he appears to suggest, is less an end in itself than an intermediary stage in a process whose end cannot be foreseen.

As the poet suggests in *Canzone* 128, "*Italia mia,*" it is not some lower class convention, but convention of a type more likely to be epitomized by the rich and powerful, in terms of which he feels constrained:

> *Canzone, io t'ammonisco*
> *che tua ragion cortesemente dica,*
> *perchè fra gente altera ir ti convene*
> *et le voglie son piene*
> *già de l'usanza pessima et antica,*
> *del ver sempre nemica.*

> Song, I bid you speak your message courteously,
> for you must go among a haughty people, and their
> wills are still full of vicious and old custom,
> always the enemy of truth. (128. 113–18)

In order to "go among" the audience to whom this *canzone* is directed, the poet suggests that he has had, to some extent, to speak their language. In doing so he himself risks falling victim to *usanza,* and becoming paralyzed for his pains by an anachronistic sense of sinfulness—*Io son si stanco sotto 'l fascio antico / de le mie colpe e de l'usanza ria* (I am so weary under the ancient bundle of my sins and bitter habit [81. 1–2]). In Sonnet 234 he appears to reverse himself, to look to the *vulgo* for refuge:

> *e'l vulgo a me nemico et odioso*
> *(chi'l pensò mai?) per mio refugio chero:*
> *tal paura ò di ritrovarmi solo.*

> and I seek (whoever thought it?) the mob,
> inimical and hateful to me, as a refuge:
> so afraid am I of being alone. (234. 12–14)

The double-edge of his poetics to which these lines call attention might be described as follows: unless this exclusive and difficult discourse becomes a collective language, the poet will find himself writing to and for no one, or worse, he will find himself isolated in the collective misunderstanding of him. Especially were he to succeed *only* to the extent of transforming "himself" in the eyes of the *vulgo* he would be playing the part of Ulysses—seeming to present an itinerary of self-willed emancipation insofar as his dependence upon an understanding of language and its interpretation different from theirs is not taken into account. He at least feigns a retreat here, in accordance with his own principles of interpretation, the better to show that the poetic project in which he is engaged would be self-defeating and self-defeated were he alone and only to escape the *vulgo.* It would be better to remain entirely within the problematic of *l'usanza pessima et antica* than to achieve such a virulent "solitude."

In other words, Petrarch's disclaimers, direct or indirect, of the value and success of his poetry are by no means disingenuous, nor need they be considered discontinuous with or contradictory to some other "stratum" of the text, as one recent commentator has argued.[29] Precisely because language itself and not the human will is the locus of deception, the poet in the

Canzoniere is more than ever accountable for what he says and does. The original error to which the *rime sparse* are retrospectively attributed in the opening sonnet still carries the sense of personal responsibility—mio *primo giovenile errore*—in addition to the philosophical sense that there is no "origin," only error, or that identity and origin will always be discoverable as a function of difference and *vaneggiar,* the free play of dream language. A similar double sense may be attached to the recurrent penitential poems scattered throughout the *Canzoniere,* not least, as I suggested in the first chapter, to *Canzone* 366, the hymn to the Virgin, which ends the sequence. Previous observations already argue that these poems are not retractions in the traditional sense—Christian palinodes to the poet's profane love and profane love poetry—denoting repentance of that first error and its consequences, and a readiness to change, to redirect his attention to his soul's salvation. Further considerations will suggest more precisely what their function and significance become in terms of the collection in which they play a part.

The opening sonnet is itself, as we have seen, perfectly ambiguous. The sense of line four—*Quand 'era in parte altr'uom da quel ch' i' sono*—could be both that the poet has undergone a conversion (as, in the historico-linguistic sense we have been investigating, he has) and precisely the opposite, that conversion is as far off as ever (which it is since the distinction between "old self" and "new self" has become indeterminate). This local ambiguity, coupled with the oddity of multiple retractions where we might have expected a single irreversible "turn," work to transmute the theme of conversion into one of the *Canzoniere's* own conventions—a convention which neatly (and arbitrarily) structures other thematic concerns of the sequence, but does not break away from them. The closing prayer to the Virgin operates in a similar way vis-à-vis the *Canzoniere's* inter-referentiality with the *Commedia.* Robert Durling has already pointed out that the conversion sought in this prayer remains contingent upon an external change, upon an act of divine intervention which fails to occur, at least within the boundaries of the sequence.[30] The answer to Petrarch's prayer is conspicuous by its absence, in part, because in *Paradiso* XXXIII Saint Bernard's prayer to the Virgin on behalf of the repentant Dante (*ll.* 1–39) *is* answered. The placement of Petrarch's address to the Virgin at the end of a long "autobiographical" poetic sequence, and the fact that always before Petrarch has addressed his penitential sighs to one of the three persons of the Trinity, suggest that Dante's lines are to some degree *the* reference for this poem. Whatever else he hopes to accomplish, the poet here simultaneously invents and places himself within a literary "tradition." Like the repetition of penitential poems within the *Canzoniere,* the repetition or imitation of prayers to the Virgin within the tradition becomes in a broad sense "conventional." By this means, what Petrarch does with the theme of conversion in his own sequence, he does to the sequence of works in a longer "literary history" as well.

Where it differs dramatically from *Paradiso* XXXIII, in imagery and poetic strategy, Petrarch's poem is conventional in a narrower sense. It imitates several of Petrarch's other *canzoni* addressed to Laura. The beautiful eyes (*l.* 22), the lady as pole star for the storm-tossed lover (*l.* 68), the reference to love as the instigator of this poetry (*l.* 4), the assurances that if the lady were to show him her favor, the poet would write differently from the way he has written up to now (*ll.* 124–28) all closely paraphrase *Canzone* 73. As in other poems to Laura, his humility is mixed with assertion. He cajoles—*ma ti prego / che'l tuo nemico del mio mal non rida* (but I beg you that your enemy may not laugh at my harm [*ll.* 74–75])—and he goes on, in fact, to recommend himself to the Virgin precisely on the grounds that he has proved himself such a faithful lover to a mortal woman: *Che se poca mortal terra caduca / amar con sí mirabil fede soglio, / che devrò far di te, cosa gentile?* (For if I am accustomed to loving transitory mortal earth with such miraculous faith, what must I do with you, a noble thing? [*ll.* 121–23]) (translation mine).

In trying to comprehend the significance of the first sonnet and the final *canzone* as well as the penitential poems in between, this complex of considerations—their thematic and stylistic consistencies with other poems in the sequence, the oddity of finding multiple "retractions" throughout the work, the function these poems serve as a thematic focusing device, and their inability to reassure us of a change of heart on the part of the poet—may be taken collectively into account. Pointing, not outward toward the life of the poet, but inward toward the text and subtexts whose boundaries they delimit, they serve notice that there is nothing disinterested about this poetic language. (The warning they provide is all the more significant precisely *because* Petrarch's poetic mode, his "pure" poetry, might seem to remove his literary production from the spheres of moral, political, philosophical, or spiritual considerations.) For if language remains the "body" of knowledge and desire, then Petrarch's refusal to "believe" language and his demonstrations of the ways in which it is not to be believed—whatever the distance he appears to maintain from the world of *usanza*—necessarily call into question everything that is to be known, thought, and felt. For all their calculation and philosophical rigor, these poems stand, at the beginning and end and throughout the sequence, as expressions of the tremendous psychological and spiritual risk to himself and to his readers involved in the transition the poet hopes he is making.

This aspect of the penitential poems does not, however, prevent them from similarly implicating *all* poetry. It is a way of reading no less than a way of writing in which Petrarch instructs us, and this way of reading is not to be confined to his text alone. His implication of Dante's text in particular is necessary, for it is Dante's allegorical mode of reading/writing which urgently demands deconstruction and revision if the transition is to be negotiated successfully. One cannot simply read one text one way and another text another way, for that, far more than Petrarch's skepticism, would be destructive of language's capacity to "make manifest," if nothing else, itself (and its history).

The history of language, especially of literary language, also necessarily changes in terms of Petrarch's new mode of reading, meaning that a further task confronting the poet, besides "conventionalizing" Dante, is to disrupt and reconceptualize the view of literary history exemplified by Dante. The full range of Petrarch's literary-historical revisionism is well beyond the range of my argument here, but a brief look at Petrarch's relationship to one of Petrarch's and Dante's mutual vernacular precursors, Arnaut Daniel, serves economically both to demonstrate the seriousness and scope of that project and to extend one step further the delineation of the significant difference between Petrarch's and Dante's presentations of the relationship between language and experience.

Arnaut, the inventor of the *sestina,* was one of the most technically innovative of the Provençal poets, and is acknowledged by both Dante and Petrarch as their greatest mentor in the craft of writing vernacular poetry. Petrarch mentions him admiringly in the *Trionfi* (*"Triumphus cupidinis,"* IV. 40–42) and alludes to several of his poems in the *Canzoniere.* Dante, who includes a *sestina* among his *rime petrose,* records his debt to Arnaut and the Provençal tradition in *Purgatorio* XXVI where Guido Guinizelli, the father, according to Dante, of the circle of Florentine love poets with whom he had once associated himself, points to Arnaut as a *miglior fabbro del parlar materno* (better craftsman of the mother tongue [*Purg.* XXVI, 117]).[31] Arnaut himself, in the *congedo* of his one surviving *sestina,* appears to regard his virtuosity as that of a clever player of a purely linguistic game, calling his poem a song "about" the near homonyms "nail" and "uncle": *Arnaut tramet sa chanson d'ongl' e d'oncle* (*Sestina,* 37).[32] Since Latin was still the language of history and theology, and vernacular poetry still something of a novelty, this characterization seems accurate. If Arnaut thought he was just playing a game, however, Dante maintains that the game is always allegorically real. Having arrived at the position that all languages are equally contingent,[33] Dante exerts great pressure on the Italian vernacular to yield up not only its phonetic and metrical secrets, but also, what has not been asked of it before, to reveal the ways in which it embodies the living reality of a history through which the truth of God's providential plan is to be grasped. This is precisely the sense of the remarkable speech in Provençal (here submitted to the dictates of *terza rima* and even made to rhyme with the surrounding Italian lines) which Dante attributes to an Arnaut who, now in Purgatory, sees the "error" of his understanding of vernacular language. Abandoning the historical Arnaut's esoteric *trobar clus* he says to Dante the pilgrim:

> *Tan m'abellis vostre cortes deman,*
> *qu'ieu no me puesc ni voill a vos cobrire.*
> *Ieu sui Arnaut, que plor e vau cantan;*

consiros vei la passada folor,
e vei jausen lo joi qu'esper, denan.

So does your courteous request please me that I neither
can nor would conceal myself from you. I am Arnaut,
who weep and sing as I go; contritely I see my
past folly, and joyously I see before me the joy
that I await. (*Purg.* XXVI, 140–47)

In part this means that, understood correctly, even Arnaut's apparently "closed," apparently nonexistential language was the
language of being. It was not "deceptive" in the Ulyssean sense
(contrary to Ulysses, Arnaut did call attention to the purely
material basis of his language), but it remains to the reader to
"open" Arnaut's poetry to its larger allegorical-historical con
text, much as the figure of Arnaut here opens himself ("I neither can nor would conceal myself from you") to the pilgrim's
courteous request.

According to Petrarch, four poets—Cavalcanti, Dante,
Cino da Pistoia, and he himself—are all Arnaut's heirs, whatever the purpose to which they put the instrument he prepared
for them. This is one sense of his *Canzone* 70, *"Lasso me ch'i
non so in qual parte pieghi,"* where each stanza ends with the
first line of a *canzone* by one of these poets. Beginning with the
first line of a *canzone* he believed to be by Arnaut, he proceeds
in chronological order, ending with the first line of his own
Canzone 23. He does not, however, try to "correct" Arnaut as
Dante does, but instead measures his distance from the Provençal master both chronologically and, difficult though this may
be under his indeterminate circumstances (he does not know
where to *turn*), ideologically. His borrowings from Arnaut here
and in other poems suggest that despite the clear genealogical
continuity of poetry, the passage of years has seen certain irreversible changes, not the least of which is that there remains no
larger allegorical-historical context into which such changes
may be translated.

We may take as a further example the conceit of an ox
chasing a hare which occurs three times in the extant poetry of
Arnaut, one of whose *cansos* ends thus:

Ieu sui Arnautz qu'amas l'aura,
E chatz la lebre ab lo bou
E nadi contra suberna.

I am Arnaut who collects the air, and chases
the hare on the ox, and swims against the tide.[34]
(*ll.* 43–45)

Petrarch adapts this conceit in Sonnet 212 and in *Sestina* 239 to
describe his pursuit of Laura:

et una cerva errante e fugitiva
caccia con un bue zoppo e 'nfermo e lento.

and I pursue a wandering fleeing doe with a
lame, sick, slow ox. (212. 7–8)

et col bue zoppo andrem cacciando l'aura.

we shall go with a lame ox hunting the air.
(translation mine) (239. 36)

Arnaut's use of the conceit appears to refer to his poetic tech-
nique, the *trobar clus,* which he developed in reaction to the
diction and imagery of other troubadour poets. He goes against
the grain or "tide" of fluent love poetry. His ingenious forms,
odd conceits, and convoluted syntax force the language of common speech to its limits, as if to lay bare the specific properties
and latent poetic possibilities of the Romance vernacular which
other poets had been discovering and using with less height-
ened complexity and self-consciousness. The sense of Arnaut's
conceit or conceits is that, despite his unorthodox methods, he
succeeds in writing love poetry. He seems to take great pleasure
in the poet's power to collect and organize an "airy" language,
to make sense emerge from sound, to reveal, through puns and
rhymes, through paradox and contradiction, the possibilities of
his medium. His paradoxes, it should be noted, illustrate the
success of his project even as they comment upon it.

Petrarch shares with Arnaut the exhilaration of knowing
his medium inside and out, but for him Arnaut's paradoxes become distressingly literal. In Sonnet 212, by taking the two dis-
cordant elements of the paradox, the slow animal of the hunter

and the swift prey, and exaggerating the distinctive characteristics of each (the "hare" becomes a swifter *cerva* which is now *errante e fugitiva,* while the ox is not only slow but lame and infirm, *zoppo e 'nfermo e lento*), Petrarch stretches the bond of simple antithesis which momentarily held them together, enacting and describing a poetics of discontinuity which separates rather than joins means and ends. As Petrarch's further separation of hunter and hunted into different lines perhaps suggests, the paradox was a fragile structure which depended upon Arnaut's assumption of a kind of self-enclosed linguistic "ground." Both of the alterations of Arnaut's conceit in Sonnet 212 register the fact that since Dante has promoted the vernacular to the status of a language of being, Petrarch, in "undoing" Dante, undoes the distinction Arnaut was making as well. The ground for the paradox is gone. Thus the sense of direction implied by Arnaut's swimming against the tide is unavailable to Petrarch who, in the opening quatrain of Sonnet 212, has first (dis)located himself in relation to Arnaut by noting that difference: *Nuoto per mar che non a fondo o riva* (I swim through a sea that has no floor or shore" [212. 3]). In other words, for Petrarch and the Petrarchan reader, Arnaut becomes as indeterminate a point of orientation as his heir(s), a poet whose compositions must "now" be read as relationally or comparatively (rather than allegorically) as Petrarch's own.

The "Structure" of the *Canzoniere*

Up to this point my readings have highlighted stylistic features and patterns of allusion in the *Canzoniere,* implying by the freedom with which I draw upon formal and thematic characteristics of various poems that the *Canzoniere* can support this kind of reading. Before proceeding further with this kind of exegesis, I would like to comment on what I take to be the procedure or process of the sequence. What we could call the mode of poetic production in the *Canzoniere* is an issue which has been hotly debated by critics, usually in the form of discussions of the *Canzoniere's* "structure." Those who find a structure tend to conclude that the poet and his poetry are ultimately products of the moral and theological codes in terms of which they situate themselves. Those who do not find a structure are more likely to see Petrarch as an innovator, as a proto-Renaissance or proto-modern figure, whose "originality" then deflects attention away from a consideration of the process of his creation. In the opening chapter we saw that an understanding of the mode of production underwriting Petrarch's concept of history was important to our being able to discuss that concept in nonidealist terms, in terms not of its relative accuracy or truth, but of how it functioned as a reflection and as a criticism of the status quo. Perhaps more importantly, this investigation allowed us to consider the provisional status such a radical revision of history must have had for Petrarch, and hence to see, in some of his most problematic writing, the process whereby a new way of organizing experience was taking shape. For similar reasons it is important to try to describe the materials and characteristics of Petrarch's poetic organization of the *Canzoniere*. In doing so, I appeal once again to Harold Bloom who recognizes in his delineation of "revisionary ratios" that the way a poet uses the materials at hand—not just his rhetorical stance, the static pose of a speaker, but the activity he performs with respect to other poets—can be his, and also our, way of producing poetic meaning.[35]

It is hardly surprising in light of the interpretive difficulties presented by the poetry of the *Canzoniere* that readers have looked for some kind of structure or patterning, governing the whole, which might anchor Petrarch's volatility and ambiguity to a purpose, if not necessarily to a resolution. But the apparently contradictory signals given in the sequence, about where or how to look for its design and what its nature might be, have traditionally been regarded as an obstacle to the discovery of that purpose. Rarely has the *Canzoniere* been taken as a pretext for revising our own assumptions about literary structure, so that Petrarch's concern for order and his equal emphasis on instability might be reconciled in our apprehension of a process accessible to analysis. Instead, in the recent history of Petrarch criticism scholars have offered equally plausible but mutually exclusive arguments which tend to be linked with a desire to place Petrarch safely inside either the Middle Ages or the modern era. It is interesting to speculate on the politics of both critical gestures. It is chiefly the "mixed metaphors" of our own mediating critical structures (Petrarch's fictive periodization of history, for example, having become second nature to us), that are tacitly ignored, left unexamined, by discounting either side in the debate. The act of choosing one side or the other avoids the uncertain or indeterminate position between the choices which would force us to become self-conscious about the ground on which we stand in order to make the choice. What one would be forced to become conscious of is that the ground for such a choice is illusory. This is precisely what I believe Petrarch's poetry is designed to do, which explains why, in one sense, its "structure" has appeared so elusive.

Petrarch's fascination with and attention to various kinds of patterning has, in itself, always been quite obvious. His own marginal comments register his awareness of such matters as how many poems up to a certain point in the sequence are sonnets. He established the proportions between the two parts of the sequence long before the total number of poems reached three hundred and sixty-six, maintaining this ratio through numerous additions and revisions.[36] Yet he also kept reordering poems and pieces of poems up until his death. If one tries to imagine exchanging a passage of *Purgatorio* for one in *Inferno,* or even transferring passages from one place to another within a canticle, then one gets some idea of the differences which might obtain among ordering principles in general. Indeed, just as one attribute of Dante's "new" rhyme scheme is that it insures against intentional or accidental interpolations and transpositions by copyists, so Petrarch's relatively autonomous, independent "old" verse forms allow and invite a certain amount or kind of reordering, not only on the part of the poet, but also on the part of the reader. It will be useful in determining the intentions and imperatives of Petrarchan patterns to take into account both sides of the critical debate on the subject, for the intricacy and hiddenness of the linkages, echoings, and significant spacings among the *Canzoniere* which have driven critics into one camp or the other, are such that no single, unaided commentator could have a sensibility broad enough to identify a full range of them.

Carlo Calcaterra and Umberto Bosco have been influential in establishing the two poles of this debate. In his series of studies, *Nella selva del Petrarca,* Calcaterra argued that the thematic evolution of the Apollo-Daphne myth provides Petrarch's principle of design, together with the superimposition of a moral and religious structure upon this design in the later poems. Thus for Calcaterra the *Canzoniere* has a plot of sorts which reflects and sets an example (meant to be followed, though Calcaterra does not say this in so many words) of a peculiarly personal redemption.[37] Umberto Bosco, on the other hand, claims in *Francesco Petrarca* that Petrarch is a poet without history or story, reasoning from Petrarch's method of composition that the *Canzoniere* is a book without narrative progression or systematic design. Petrarch's love for Laura, the moving center of the sequence, he argues, remains always identical to itself at whatever point one sees it. If there is a tendency toward a narrative shape, it would be that of a psychological novel, but he feels that Petrarch fails to achieve that shape due to his own technical inadequacies.[38]

These two positions reflect or repeat an ambivalence we have just seen in the text. The penitential poems pointed to the presence of narrative elements, and to their inability to constitute a narrative. In the discussion above we saw that they worked thematically to structure whatever narrative there was, and yet by their number and location they indicated their own failure to achieve a nonparticipation in that narrative, the nonparticipation upon which narrative progression and closure would have depended. The miscalculation that Calcaterra and Bosco have in common is their premature thematizing of a text in which thematics are deemphasized and qualified by means of the prominence given to the *deployment* of thematic elements. Neither is prepared to see that it is narrative itself that Petrarch must call into question if he is to place the points of reference that prevent the telling of his own story. Bosco's sense of a moving center and Calcaterra's recognition of a double plot, though, are not themselves discredited by the critical framework within which they are presented. Rather, together they contribute to a characterization of the generative mechanisms of the *Canzoniere* that will necessarily shift attention away from the story per se as the object of study.

More recently Aldo Scaglione and Thomas Roche have presented studies of the workings of the *Canzoniere* which complicate further the narrative vs. non-narrative opposition. In addition to overlapping somewhat with Bosco's non-narrative reading of Petrarch, Scaglione is also oriented toward recent literary theory, especially to Umberto Eco's discussion of the *opera aperta*.[39] Scaglione does not detect in Petrarch's method of composition or in the text as we have it any failure of poetic skill, but a formalism which eschews linear progression and closure, which systematically cultivates indeterminacy and instability: ". . . it would not be illegitimate to read Petrarch as the announcer of 'modern' positions, taking account of his artistic forms and their relationship with his psychology of methodical ambiguity and his vision of a contradictory and dissociated world."[40] This description provides a more exacting guide than does Bosco's to the reading of the *Canzoniere* because it refuses to discount any aspect of the work, and insists upon a relationship between poetics and *Weltanschauung*. I would qualify Scaglione's position, though, by suggesting that it will take us farther if we distinguish "the world" from the symbolic systems mediating human understanding of the world. Petrarch's concern with these systems, of course, seems to draw upon his sense of contemporary dissolution and upheaval, but that same concern, as I explained in the opening chapter, moots the question of his world view. The myth of his times which Petrarch sometimes claims as the determinant of his writing, is itself implicated in the indeterminacy of the language with which it is described. The idea of an open work, though, can be imported completely into the sphere of the poet's linguistic possibilities. If Petrarch's artistic forms are attributed to a vision not of a *world* but of a *language* which is contradictory and dissociated, then it becomes possible to search for a pattern which is at once "open" and historically specific, a pattern which does not limit the oscillations and indeterminacies of language (and of the interpretation of that language), but which nevertheless enacts a self-recognition specific to a particular time and place in literature (which is to say a time and place whose position relative to the reader cannot be fixed, but can be continually reassessed). As Scaglione recognizes, if this poetry is conceptually open-ended, then its interpretation, too, must be considered an on-going process.[41]

Thomas Roche, on the other hand, who has recently described a complex "calendrical structure," has reanimated some of Calcaterra's claims.⁴² The design Roche has elucidated, whereby the first poem in the sequence is taken to correspond to the poet's *inamoramento* on Good Friday, and *Canzone 264*, the first poem of the *Seconda parte*, with Christmas, leads him to suggest that the *Canzoniere* remain firmly embedded in the medieval opposition between earthly love, *cupiditas*, and divine love, *caritas:* the death of Christ corresponds metaphorically to the birth of love for Laura and the birth of Christ to the death of Laura. The Good Friday-Christmas dating of 1 and 264, furthermore, allows the discovery of several instances where the punctuation of series of sonnets by *canzoni, ballate, sestine,* and *madrigali* correspond to other significant dates in the liturgical year. After working this model of the *Canzoniere's* structure up to the point where it operates as a composite calendar for three actual years claimed by Petrarch to have particular significance in his emotional and spiritual development—1327, the year he fell in love with Laura, 1341, the year of his coronation as poet laureate, and 1348, the year Laura died—Roche concludes that the liturgical scheme is meant to be the definitive interpretive context for Petrarch's life or fictionalized life, as we have it in the sequence. Citing Dante's use of numerological structuring and the theories of the mathematical basis of the universe held by Dante's contemporaries as analogues, he claims that literary history indicates the interpretive priority which this scheme should take over the "events of experience" which it counterpoints.⁴³

It is not impossible, though, to turn the entire argument around, particularly the final point, and to see in Roche's process of discovery, if not in his inferences, an elegant corroboration of the opposite, non-narrative and astructural view held by Bosco and Scaglione. If my brief presentation and discussion of these other critics have been sufficient to suggest the direction in which a more productive consideration of the *Canzoniere's* "structure" might move, Roche's argument will lead us to a more extensive investigation of a particular aspect of this "structure." In searching for and finding a calendrical framework, Roche has turned up a variety of intricate number games which suggest that Petrarch calculatingly breaks with his predecessors on the matter of number. Petrarch seems to find numbers no more reassuring than he does linguistic signs, and he uses them in ways comparable to the ways he uses language. The calendrical design, for instance, is built up of other ordering and structuring devices which are reminiscent of the self-reflexive order of the *sestina* as we have considered it earlier. The patterning of three madrigals that provides an important clue to Roche's "larger" discovery will illustrate this. Quite rightly Roche asks, "Is it mere coincidence that the number of the first two (52 and 54) *add up* to the number of the third (106) and that *Canzone* 53 contains 106 lines?" (emphasis mine).[44] Elsewhere he notes: "Of the self-dating poems (30, 50, 62, 79, 101, 118, 122, 145, 212, 266, 271, 278, 364) all are sonnets except for the first two. Number 30, a *sestina*, is the seventh non-sonnet in the sequence and contains the phrase 'oggi ha sett'anni,' the seventh anniversary of his first sight of Laura. Number 50, the fifth *canzone* and the ninth non-sonnet of the sequence contains the phrase 'ben presso al decim'anno.' "[45] To give a third example of Petrarch's additive strategy, *Canzone* 323 repeats the theme of metamorphosis and the six-part thematic structure of *Canzone* 23.

These internal relationships, the stuff of Petrarch's calendar, are derived, theoretical mathematics tells us, from the number one (by means of the addition of ones). It is impossible to say whether Petrarch is building up a theologically resonant structure from the operations of the system of whole numbers, or resolving it back into its constituent mathematical functions. The result is the same: the provocative numbering of the poems (366 incites the reader as boldly as Laura's beauty does the poet) lures the reader into looking for some kind of calendar, certainly, but the means by which this fictional calendar is constituted (by the reader, and inferentially by the poet) calls into question its authority to articulate human experience. Time, or the way it is known here, is rendered suspect as a way of demarcating events and of organizing them in relation to each other because the numerological scheme in terms of which it is figured is at once arbitrary and self-referential. Most striking of all are the differences between the way this numerological scheme "works" and the way Dante's does. It is in terms of these differences that I would like to locate an appropriate context for further discussion of the "structure" of the *Canzoniere*, particularly as it is numerically identified.

Dante finesses the problem of the arbitrary nature of number systems by basing his mathematics not on one but on three (3, 3^2 or 9, and $3^2 + 1$ or ten seem to be his points of orientation numerically). *Inferno*, for instance, has three beginnings— Canto I, the prologue, Canto II, the meeting with Vergil, Canto III, the entrance into hell—as if to indicate that the order which follows is at once relative and to be located relatively (in much the same sense that we have seen the language of the poem to be relative). The poem *qua* poem has no unitary point of origin. The number three, aside from its traditional doctrinal significance, also has some special properties. It is the smallest prime number which signifies a relationship of more than one dimension. That is, the relationship of two points to each other can be stabilized only by the introduction of a third, as in a triangle. Thus three has a kind of metamathematical dimension, showing how the elements which constitute it operate in terms of each other. Put another way, the addition of one and one calls for a third term to complete and comment upon the process of generating two from one. The interlocking of threes of Dante's *terza rima* and the repetitive rather than consecutive ordering of the cantos in each of the three canticles call attention to the fact that it is the metamathematical property of the number three rather than (or as well as) a traditional significance that is being invoked. The poem is geometrically organized, not according to the indefinite additive process which forms the basis of Petrarch's numerical design, but according to a definite, though circular, process whereby the relationships between particular numbers are understood in terms of the operational principle which makes the entire system intelligible. By means of the mathematical strategy of adding one dimension to another and discovering the parameters of the first in relation to the second (precisely the operation figured in the number three and analogous to a linguistic strategy of altering poetics in each of the three canticles),[46] Dante's conceptual apparatus at a certain point "transcends" the metaphors of time and (Euclidean) space. But by showing that this "transcendence" depends upon all the steps which precede it, the poem does not so much call into question as affirm the epistemological value of number itself, number understood as a *via,* as a means, and not numbers or numerical symmetries taken to be ends in themselves.

I will explain what I mean by "transcendence" with reference to the extraordinary augmentation of dimension which occurs in *Paradiso* XXVIII, where Dante's conceptual apparatus absorbs and moves beyond three-dimensional space, a figure which deeply conditions human knowledge (and our understanding of the nature of that knowledge). The final figure in the poem for the shape of the universe is, appropriately, a three-sphere, a figure which can most easily be described as a sphere in four dimensions.[47] Dante's exchange with Beatrice concerning the relationship of this figure to the three-dimensional spherical cosmos through which he has been ascending is the poet's most explicit commentary on the epistemological efficacy not of number per se, but of mathematical thought. The situation is this: the pilgrim, from the perspective of the *ciel velocissimo,* which seems to be at the outermost edge of the cosmos (Singleton comments, "The ninth heaven, or Primum Mobile, which contains no bodies, neither stars nor planets, but is the outermost of the moving spheres, imparting its motion to the rest."[48]), is confronted with a vision of a dimensionless but blindingly piercing point on which, Beatrice informs him, the heaven and all nature depend. The point is surrounded by ever-widening concentric circles, the smallest and fastest of which "intruths" itself most in the "pure spark" or *favilla pura.*[49] The problem presented by this vision is that in the material universe, or what Dante more accurately calls *il mondo sensibile* (*Par.* XXVIII, 49), the world of sense, celestial spheres appear to move more swiftly and to be more approximate to the "truth" the larger they are and the more remote they are from their center. Considering the circumstances, that the pilgrim sees as if in the distance the "place" in the universe where he is himself "standing," he remains remarkably calm, even stolid. It remains for the reader to do the double-take upon realizing that there suddenly seem to be two *cieli velocissimi.*

Curiously, though the pilgrim can think of, or at least utter, linguistic analogues for the relationship between the familiar geocentric cosmos and the new configuration, he cannot

work out the necessary mathematical operation that would make
sense of it:

> *Onde, se 'l mio disir dee aver fine*
>   *in questo miro e angelico templo*
>   *che solo amore e luce ha per confine,*
> *udir convienmi ancor come l'essemplo*
>   *e l'essemplare non vanno d'un modo,*
> *ché io per me indarno a ciò contemplo.*

> Wherefore if my desire is to attain its end
> in this wondrous and angelic temple which has
> only love and light for its confine, needs must
> I further hear why the model and the copy go
> not in one fashion, for by myself I contemplate
> this in vain. (*Par.* XXVIII, 52–57)

Earlier spatial imagery and this final revelation—the last instance in which the terrain that Dante has to traverse is described spatially—are related not as microcosm to macrocosm,
as copy to original, or as part to whole, all of which are relationships in which the same coordinates govern both terms, but
as *l'essemplo* to *l'essemplare*. *L'essemplare*, as it is used here,
resists both English translation and conventional Italian usage.
As a noun *l'essemplare* means model or pattern, but juxtaposed
to the noun *l'essemplo*, which is etymologically the same but
denotatively different (literally, "the example"), the former
regains its infinitive force. The relationship, then, as construed
linguistically by Dante, is like that between the example and the
process or capability of producing the example, two incommensurable, though obviously interdependent propositions. As these
two propositions do not share the same semantic ground despite
their equally nominative appearance, so the two cosmic figures
do not share the same space despite their apparent geometrical
congruence. Similarly, there is a qualitative difference between
templo, the figure Dante is asked to come to terms with, and
contemplo, the intellectual and spiritual activity which right-
fully is undertaken in a *templo* but which should transcend that
setting or occasion. In other words, the process or capability
which he is called upon to understand is still not an end in it-

self, but becomes, in turn, the setting or occasion for further "contemplation."

The aptness of Dante's linguistic analogues shows that his difficulty with the corresponding mathematical operation is what mathematicians call an "inessential" one. (He knows *what* he must do; he simply cannot do it.) Beatrice's comment on this inessential difficulty attributes the shortcomings of Dante's geometry to history rather than to some flaw in the geometry itself:

> Se li tuoi diti non sono a tal nodo
> sufficienti, non è maraviglia;
> tanto, per non tentare, è fatto sodo!

> If your fingers are insufficient for such
> a knot, it is no wonder, so hard has it
> become by not being tried. (*Par.* XXVIII, 58–60)

The pilgrim's intuitive reification of the terms—up/down, near/far, large/small, etc.—in which material things are understood and evaluated, his instinctive search for a quantitative *correspondence* between material space and the space of eternity, even though he also understands, even before Beatrice explains, that the relationship is one of qualitative *consequence*, register as graphically as any of the polemics in the *Commedia* the consequences, in Dante's view, of the abdication by spiritual leaders of their role in guiding and shaping human thought. The operation of the poem here, on the other hand, realizes and retrospectively illuminates Dante's apparent pretensions to prophetic utterance, as I shall explain in a moment.

In order to free Dante of his historically conditioned habit of mind, Beatrice has shown him the pattern and measure of the three-dimensional universe, and now explains to him in rigorous terms the relative nature of his means of taking measurement and of reading the significance of the pattern. She suggests that he detach his measure from one property, *la parvenza* or the appearance, and reattach it to another property, the *virtù* of what she calls *le sustanze* or substances:

> . . . costui che tutto quanto rape
> l'altro universo seco, corrisponde
> al cerchio che più ama e che più sape:
> per che, se tu a la virtù circonde

la tua misura, non a la parvenza
de le sustanze che t'appaion tonde,
tu vederai mirabil consequenza
di maggio a più e di minore a meno
in ciascun cielo, a sua intelligenza.

. . . this sphere [where she and Dante are
positioned] which carries along with it all of
the other universe, corresponds to the circle
which loves most and knows most: because, if
you surround the virtue with your measure, not
the appearance of the substances which appear to
you round, you will see a wonderful consequence
of greater to more and of smaller to less, in
each sphere, according to its intelligence.
(translation mine) (*Par.* XXVIII, 70–78)

What Beatrice is saying is entirely comprehensible algebraically,
and is, in fact, a kind of moral algebra. As diagrammed in the
appended note, we can detach value from the coordinates of
three-dimensional space and move beyond the physics of a two-
sphere to that of a three-sphere. We have exactly the same difficulty Dante does trying to visualize the relationship between a
two-sphere and a three-sphere, but this is precisely the virtue of
making the transition. In working out our equations beyond the
limits of "intuitive" comprehension, we also come to understand intimately the self-referential, nonmimetic character of
such mathematical operations and the metaphorical nature of
the numbers they generate. This is not the same as to say that
mathematical measure is inaccurate. Euclidean geometry (which
is, of course, no more intuitive than any other except by convention) is not discredited by topology and relativity theory; on
the contrary, once its limits are circumscribed and defined by a
new geometry, it becomes more accurate than it was when its
axioms were taken to be universal. A moment's reflection will
reveal that it is the self-consistent but open-ended nature of
mathematical thought which, in fact, allows these limits to be
discovered and which ultimately allows our model of the universe to "transcend" matter, too. In both cases, ours and
Dante's, material reality *must* be transcended if, and in the
sense that, it is to be known *completely* as it functions in terms

of the mathematical categories being used to interpret it. Otherwise that knowledge is compromised by a possible confusion between the properties of the signifier and those of the signified. The objective is not to frame a picture of the universe, but a picture of our understanding of the universe.

Dante very carefully throughout *Paradiso* works to maintain this exegetical pressure, especially in his use of theological doctrine. Over and over again, the pilgrim is faced with situations which seem to abrogate Church doctrine, only to be shown by Beatrice or some other celestial interlocutor that what appears to be a contradiction of doctrine is a consequence of his own wooden application of a system which, understood and used correctly, both illuminates and is illuminated by the anomalous situation. Though neither his linguistic nor his numerical system need be any the less fictive, any the less arbitrary, than those of Petrarch, they are not simply self-referential in the additively indefinite, but dimensionally finite sense that Petrarchan numbers and letters are. John Freccero, in his study of Petrarch's poetics, notes in passing the relevance of Augustine's distinction between things to be used (*uti*) and things to be enjoyed (*frui*) to a discussion of the differences in semiotic practice between Dante and Petrarch. According to Augustine, Freccero writes, sin "consists in enjoying that which should be used," and since God alone is to be enjoyed, all other things (including signs) are to be used. In linguistic terms, "to deprive signs of their referentiality [which Freccero has established as referentiality to other signs] and to treat a poetic statement as autonomous, an end in itself, is idolatry."[50] The continual *askesis* of Dante's poetry is designed or intended to preclude (although it cannot prevent) its being read in an idolatrous manner. As my digression on the nature of Dante's numerology was intended to make clear, Dante's mathematical thinking is consistent with his poetics; numbers must be used according to the same rules of symbolization as language, and vice versa, in order for neither one to be willfully deceptive. The complex alignment of two disparate symbolic systems—language and numbers—allows each to serve as check and balance to the other. The *dottrina* would be (has been, according to Beatrice) crippled by an idolatrous application of number and cosmology. Conversely the four-dimensional "universe" would be simply a mind-boggling idol were it not for its correspondence to a revivified *dottrina*. It is in this kind of "sense," I would argue, that Dante makes good his claim to be a new prophet.[51]

It is perhaps easier to countenance the idea that Petrarch is exploring the possibility of finding or inventing new rules of linguistic signification, or that he is disaffected from the metaphysics of Dante's poetics, than that he is in a similar position vis-à-vis mathematics. Dante's "new math" may be too much like the speculative mathematics upon which much modern science relies to seem vulnerable to poetic revision. Nevertheless, historians of science are beginning to urge a reconsideration of the structure of scientific thought, something like the reconsideration of poetic structure that the study of poetic influence entails.[52] The light that scientific revisionism might shed on poetic revisionism is well beyond the scope of our discussion here, but clearly it is necessary and legitimate to ask, without assuming beforehand that all poetic numerology operates the same way, why Petrarch coordinates the ordering of some of the poems in the *Canzoniere* as he does. Why should this poet go to all the trouble of embedding a sophisticated calendrical structure in the *Canzoniere,* if it is to be so esoteric that only rarely would a reader with exactly the right background and predisposition come along to find it, and if, once found, its status in the text, let alone outside it, is immediately called into question by the process through which it is constituted (adding dimensionless ones to an indeterminate, dimensionless one). To take the second part of the question first, Roche's calendrical structure is analogous (thematically as well as interpretively) to the final hymn to the Virgin. Each appears to complete an interpretive process, which, upon closer examination, it can be said merely to participate in. It is worth mentioning Roche's comment that his calendrical framework will not account for all the formal breaks in the sequence, that fifteen percent of the non-sonnets are not implicated in his scheme.[53] One might argue that this "extra" poetic material lends the design a statistically significant quantitative as well as qualitative incompleteness, that even spatially the calendar is not the context of the poetic sequence, but the sequence the context of the calendar. Why the calendar is there at all, and why it runs backward (from the anniversary of the death of Christ rather than from the anniversary of His birth) are questions I shall address more fully in the next section of this discussion.

There is a further number-related pattern discoverable in the *Canzoniere* which does not promise absolute numerological significance or some means to knowledge, but which by accident or design corresponds to the features of Petrarch's poetics which most concern us here. I do not find this pattern "essential" to the reading of the *Canzoniere,* but since it has not been commented upon before, I would nonetheless suggest its possible significance in light of these other features. Of the three hundred and sixty-six poems in the sequence, thirty-eight of them are "long" poems, which is to say they are *canzoni* and *sestine* rather than sonnets, *ballate,* or *madrigali.* Of those thirty-eight, the pillars of the sequence, so to speak, four are not concerned with Laura or the poet's relationship to her. *Canzoni* 28, 53, 119, and 128 are devoted instead to political themes, and to subjects like glory and virtue. There are, then, exactly thirty-four long poems (if one counts the final *canzone* to the Virgin) which deal with the poet's desire—exactly the same number as there are cantos in *Inferno.* The sequence in this sense, as in others we have noted, seems to "mirror" *Inferno.* The metaphor of the mirror image is borne out by the distribution of these poems. They are, in order, 22, 23, 29, 30, 37, 50, 66, 70, 71, 72, 73, 80, 105, 125, 126, 127, 129, 135, 142, 206, 207, 214, 237, 239, 264, 268, 270, 323, 325, 331, 332, 359, 360, 366. Twenty-four of them occur in the *Seconda parte,* and *Canzone* 264 marks the division between the two parts. It is in Canto IX *Inferno* that Dante the pilgrim encounters the threat of the Medusa at the wall of the City of Dis, an incident that divides his journey into very much the same proportions that Petrarch observes.

Petrarch's mirror, of course, reverses Dante's order, so that the *Canzoniere* ends, in a sense, where *Inferno* begins. Nevertheless, it is not the case, as Robert Durling has suggested, that in the last *canzone,* "Petrarch is *still* where Dante was at the beginning of the *Commedia*—turning his back on the darkness, struggling out of the water with laboring breath, yearning to climb the mountain, but unable to make it on his own" (emphasis mine).[54] A mirror reflection does not simply repeat a pattern, especially the pattern of writing. It alters the direction in which writing may be read (right to left instead of left to right), or rather necessitates that the writing be read both ways. The reader must already be reading, or trying to read, from left to right in order to grasp the new principle of reading from right to left, and will probably attempt to rearrange the letters and words again from left to right as he achieves some facility in this unaccustomed activity. The reading process is further complicated by the fact that the shapes of individual letters, as well as the order of letters in words and the order of words in lines, are reversed. The very unit of reading changes; it becomes the letter rather than the word (the Letter rather than the Word). Thus, if what the mirror reflection lacks in "substance" can be said to be made up for by the skill it requires of its reader, Petrarch's poetry, in certain respects, both precedes and exceeds Dante's *Inferno*. The sequence precedes (is prior to or more basic than) *Inferno* because its unit of reading and writing is more elementary; it exceeds (is more comprehensive or inclusive than) Dante's first canticle because it calls for a kind of reading inclusive of, but different from and not reducible to, that called for in *Inferno*. (If *Inferno* is taken in isolation from the other two canticles, then even the question of "substantiality" is mooted, Infernal discourse being itself a kind of inverse image of divine discourse.) But the mirror image which helps locate that which it images, stands precisely where the latter *is not*. If the indications of one numerical pattern in the *Canzoniere* are borne out by other aspects of the sequence, then Petrarch by no means simply repeats Dante's struggle out of the water, and, furthermore, his point of nearest tangency with Dante's beginning situation cannot be said to have any more duration in the *Canzoniere* than Dante's beginning has in the *Commedia*.

The pattern I have described and the suggestions for interpretation that it raises are still not inclusive of, but rather included in, the *Canzoniere*. As I mentioned earlier, even the class of longer poems, to say nothing of the three hundred and twenty-eight shorter ones, overflows the design. This is, I believe, a significant feature of all the structuring devices in the *Canzoniere:* there is always a *reste* or remainder in the Petrarchan structure. Other significant features are their variety and a subtlety or absence of emphasis which almost makes one doubt they are there. They are, in fact, not there in the sense that the term "structure" tends to suggest. Joseph Barber, in a recent demonstration of two, more localized patterns implicit in Petrarch's use of rhyme schemes, adduces these patterns as evidence of further sub-designs within the whole, but postpones the decision as to whether there is or is not an overall structure with a warning: "the subtle, 'hidden' nature of these patterns suggests that if there is one all encompassing scheme to the number and order of the poems in the *Canzoniere,* it may well be far more complex than has been assumed in the past."[55] This complex overall design would seem, in fact, to be none other than the very incompleteness and indefiniteness beyond which each of several readers has tried to look in the case of his own particular structural discovery. Though each of the patterns discussed here is significant, it is the reading of the patterns more than the bare fact of discovering them that is instructive. This is as true of Dante as it is of Petrarch, as my reading of Dante's numerology was intended to indicate, but it should be equally clear that the modes of reading or reading habits called for by Dante and Petrarch respectively are significantly different. Petrarch's patterning devices do not imply poetic transcendence, and it is therefore fitting that no one of them emerges as the kind of structure or pattern which organizes significance hierarchically or recursively—that, in fact, no one of them *emerges.*

If we go on to insist that without these properties, the patterns in question cannot properly be considered "literary structures," that their partial and hidden nature implies a lack of artistic control, or a failure heretofore by readers to discover *the* structure, then we are implicitly insisting that structure or structuration must be, or appear to be, transcendent in order to be significant. If we stop at calling the *Canzoniere* an "open work," on the other hand, without regard to structures which have been and may yet be identified, then we implicitly take the position that it is possible for a poetics not to have a particular structure, and by implication that our own interpretive position may be free of structural presuppositions. My reading of the *Canzoniere* has suggested that structuring elements and patterns may have immanent textual significance without implying the

ideal or transcendental structures of artistic perfection, referential sanction, or absolute interpretation. Instead (as the history of Petrarch criticism shows), the "structure" of the *Canzoniere* serves to bring to the fore the reader's own structural
presuppositions.

History—"Narrative"—Language

The "structure" of the *Canzoniere,* considered thematically, I would argue, resembles what Paul de Man has called
"the movement of ironic consciousness."[56] The term and our
valuation of the perspective it names are anachronistic, perhaps,
in a discussion of fourteenth-century poetry, but its structure, as
de Man describes it, apparently is not. He writes:

> The moment the innocence or authenticity of our
> sense of being in the world is put into question, a far
> from harmless process gets underway. It may start as
> a casual bit of play with a stray loose end of the
> fabric, but before long the entire texture of the self is
> unraveled and comes apart. The whole process hap-
> pens at an unsettling speed. Irony possesses an in-
> herent tendency to gain momentum and not to stop
> until it has run its full course; from the small and ap-
> parently innocuous exposure of a small self-deception
> it soon reaches the dimensions of the absolute.[57]

In trying to determine whether or not there is any progression
in a developmental sense in the *Canzoniere,* critics, as we have
observed, have generally looked for, and found or not found, a
"plot." Either explicitly or implicitly, within the poems or between the poems, something must happen to the poet or he
must make something happen, if only by taking a stand toward
what seems to be happening to him, if the sequence is to have
a paradigmatic shape in terms of which each of the poems could
be understood. As we have seen, the retraction poems, which
might have served to assimilate the *Canzoniere* to the self's allegorical manifestation of the plot of universal history, do not so
serve, although this plot continues to hover in the background

giving point to its nonfulfillment. If, instead of looking for such an event or stand, we focus on a different kind of pattern—the play of identity and difference (which, as we are about to see, manifests itself on a broader thematic plane as well as imagistically over the course of a few poems and structurally in individual poems) and the progressive insolubility of self-interpretive problems present from the beginning of the *Canzoniere*—then what we find is a kind of ironic progression which puts out of the question the arrival at an end point, the achievement of a privileged position from which to survey the total picture. The opening line of Sonnet 15, *Io mi rivolgo in dietro a ciascun passo* (I turn back at each step [15. 1]), aptly characterizes this movement. What appear to be breakthroughs in one sense, poems or a series of poems which isolate and work through a particular facet of the Petrarchan situation, may seem (to the poet) to hold out some hope of resolution, but they invariably succeed only in raising the unraveling process to a new level of awareness.

We have noticed, for example, that between Sonnets 49 and 170 the problem of the poet's own inability to speak escalates into a dilemma of universal proportions. There are as well a number of poems, dispersed at irregular intervals, but having in common the leitmotif of a ship at sea, which chart the "development" of the *Canzoniere* precisely as a reverse voyage—not the reverse of just any voyage, but that voyage of self-discovery which for Dante begins with a tired swimmer and ends safely in port. This group of poems also demonstrates in extended form the technical valences with which Petrarch's poetry can weight the most ordinary words, partly, as in the case of the *sestina,* by embedding them in a restricted linguistic structure, and not because of their congruence with any assumed referential structure. Though the motif of the ship progresses in a sequential order over the course of the poems in which we actually find the term *nave,* even the narrative status of this "progression" is destabilized by other poems in which the motif is merely implicit.

The voyage motif is introduced by Sonnet 26, which tells of the happy landing of a battered ship to which the poet compares himself when he discovers that his lord, Love, is no longer a victim of armed resistance:

Più di me lieta non si vede a terra
nave da l'onde combattuta et vinta . . .

. . . .
. . . veggendo quella spada scinta
che fece al segnor mio sì lunga guerra.

More glad than I, was never ship come to land
after being battled and conquered by the waves.
. . . now that I see put back in its sheath
that sword which made so long war on my lord.
(26. 1–2, 7–8)

In *Sestina* 80 the situation is more precarious. Having set out
under favorable conditions—*L'aura soave, a cui governo et*
vela / commisi entrando a l'amorosa vita (The soft breeze, to
whom I entrusted both sail and tiller, entering upon this amo-
rous life . . . [80. 7–8])—the poet finds that his vessel is less
adequate and the conditions more unfavorable than he origi-
nally supposed. He is on the high seas where not only the
treacherous waves and dangerous cliffs threaten his life, but also
his own frail bark, at first a *picciol legno* (80. 3) and later a
fraile legno (80. 28):

Et le cagion' del mio doglioso fine
non pur d'intorno avea, ma dentro al legno.
Chiuso gran tempo in questo cieco legno
errai . . .

And the causes of my sorrowful end I had, not
only all around, but also within the ship.
Shut up a long time in this blind ship . . . (80. 11–13)

In the *congedo,* however, despite the impossibility of locating
the lover's problem either "inside" or "outside" his means of
navigation, he still expresses the hope that his boat, with some
divine guidance, will carry him into port:

Signor de la mia fine et de la vita,
prima ch'i' fiacchi il legno tra li scogli,
drizza a buon porto l'affannata vela.

Lord of my death and of my life: before
I shatter my ship on these rocks direct to
a good port my weary sail. (80. 37–39)

By Sonnet 189 shipwreck seems imminent and the poet begins to despair of reaching port. His ship is sailing blindly between Scylla and Charybdis, piloted by Love whom he has come to take as his enemy, and rigged with tired shrouds drawn up by error and ignorance. *Morta fra l'onde è la ragion e l'arte* (Dead among the waves are reason and skill [189. 13]).[58] Then in Sonnet 235 even this unpromising direction and tattered rigging are lost, and the ship is completely disabled: *Disarmata di vele et di governo* (bereft of sails and tiller [235. 14]). Finally, in *Canzone* 268, the fourth poem of the *Seconda parte* of the *Canzoniere* and the first following the announcement of Laura's death, the poet (and Love) are shipwrecked: *ad uno scoglio / avrem rotto la nave* (we have wrecked our ship on the same rock [268. 15–16]),

This is not, of course, the end point, either of the story of the poet's love for Laura or of the way Petrarch has written poetry up to now. As the work of Ernest Hatch Wilkins on the dates of composition of the *Canzoniere* has shown, the division of the sequence into parts, now often referred to as *In vita* and *In morte,* actually antedated Laura's death by a year.[59] In other words, the form of the collection reflects, not the poet's reaction to an external event, but, more accurately, a shift to what I have called a "new level of awareness." This, in different terms, has also been Aldo Bernardo's interpretation of the evidence. Although Bernardo's discussion of Wilkins' work remains bound to the thematics of the *Canzoniere,* it nonetheless presents an important distinction between logical and chronological events:

> The second form, put together just one year before Laura's death, clearly reflects the start of the conflict that was to plague Petrarch throughout the remainder of his life, namely, whether his love of Laura, with all it implied, could only lead to ultimate damnation. It was this conflict, rather than the death of Laura, that apparently determined the basic form of the collection at this stage since the two parts are clearly delineated here for the first time with the introduction of poem No. 1, providing a distinct recantation of the poet's love, and No. 264, defining the inescapable

pull of that love despite the poet's strong awareness
of its negative implications for ultimate salvation.[60]

The death of Laura is fortuitous to this alteration, and, unlike
the death of Beatrice in the *Vita Nuova,* does not inaugurate a
change of the sort necessary to the process of integrating and
transcending the past. Any such change is belied by the negative fate of the ship metaphor in *Canzone* 268, as well as
by the nondifferentiation of the two parts which this motif
establishes.

However, we may also notice the ease with which a logical
development can look like a chronological development. Though
attenuated, and inverted vis-à-vis Dante, even the "plot" of the
ship assumes the shape of a narrative when it is presented dia-
chronically, as I have done. But other poems, such as Sonnet
212, where the poet is already swimming fifty-six poems before
the ship founders, implicitly subvert the diachrony of this plot,
indicating that the shipwreck describes not an "event" which
"happens," but the synchronic implications, worked out dia-
chronically, of the same and apparently unalterable situation.
Much like a cartoon character who continues to run even after
he has overshot the edge of the cliff, and falls only when he
notices the empty space below him, the poet is already a help-
less castaway in Sonnet 212, but continues sailing until he
"knows" that he is shipwrecked in *Canzone* 268. It is interesting to note in this regard that these two particular poems may
have been written within a year of each other, though their relatively wide separation from each other in the sequence works
spatially to offset any temporal association.[61] At the same time
that the subterranean relationship between the two poems deconstructs the narrative structure of the ship "plot," their relative positions further distinguish between the temporality of
language—the diachronic dimension of presentation—and "historical development."

This distinction—between narrative and history—is an
essential element, as I have argued in the first chapter, of both
Petrarch's concept of history and his poetics. Consistent with
this distinction is his treatment of *literary* history in *Canzone*
70, where he (of necessity) leaves his predecessors in their

original "written" form, in contrast to Dante's procedure in *Purgatorio* XXVI where figures in the vernacular tradition are made to "speak" in terms of their supposed underlying providential significance. Petrarch's treatment of Dante in this *canzone* is the apparent exception that proves the rule of literal fidelity to a "written" literary past (he quotes, rather than the *Commedia,* the first line of one of Dante's *rime petrose,* a poetic experiment whose strategies more closely resemble Petrarch's own and run counter to the direction taken in the *Commedia*). The possibility of reading history figuratively—and therefore narratively—is shown to be unavailable in Petrarch's construction of a different poetics of history. The repetition of the *capoverso* of *Canzone* 23 at the end of *Canzone* 70 points us back to Petrarch's own earlier poem for an extended meditation on narrative structure which further justifies *Canzone* 70's new ("old" for Dante) literary history, especially as it emerges within the structure of its figural alternative, and from the absence of this alternative as an available option.[62] This *canzone* is among the richest and longest of the poems in the *Canzoniere,* and even a partial reading of the whole poem would be excessively lengthy. A close reading of the first stanza and part of the second must suffice here to unfold the literary historical import of the poet's transformation into the laurel discussed earlier.

Canzone 23 is the poet's own attempt or demonstration of an attempt to tell the story and hence the "meaning" of his poetic activity. As Adelia Noferi has pointed out, the *canzoni* in the sequence present the problem of duration and development in a way which the highly architectural sonnets and *sestine* avoid, this first *canzone* differing from subsequent ones in presenting itself narratively "with a thread of temporal progression which is continuous and novelistic."[63] Following it, via an intermediary stage of extended declarative *canzoni,* the form, as she says, "frees" itself from narrative structure and approaches more closely the lyric quality of the sonnets. Such a transformation is not arbitrary. In *Canzone* 23 the poetics of narrative is, in a sense, exhausted, and Petrarch's *canzoni* are driven or freed, depending upon how one chooses to look at it, to assume a different shape.

A first question to be asked of this *canzone* by the narrative reader might be why it is necessary at all. Have we not been sufficiently informed by the first twenty-two poems, which this *canzone* seems in many ways to recapitulate, of the significant events and observations in the poet's career up to this point? Does not the poet himself who wrote those first twenty-two poems know what they mean? Apparently the answer to both questions is no. We have already uncovered the impossibility of pinning this poetry down in the sense of finding in it a stable, coherent set of inter-related elements. It is fitting that *Canzone* 23 is immediately preceded by the first *sestina* of the sequence, the *sestina* being the verse form which strikingly crystallizes the tension between thematic content and linguistic structure.

The stated reason for writing the poem is the expectation that by being reconstituted in language, the poet's accumulated grief will be "disembittered"—*perché cantando il duol si disacerba* (because, singing, the pain is disembittered [23. 4]). Throughout Dante's *Commedia, acerbo* and its opposite *maturo* are used consistently to describe the sinful or immature preconversion self and the virtuous, fully-realized redeemed self respectively. *Disacerba,* then, does not suggest the possibility of redemption and resolution, of finding an authentic language in which to describe an authentic experience, in the Dantesque sense. Instead it suggests an undoing of the poet's undoing which may, and in fact does, leave him as far from wholeness of being as ever. De Man's analysis of ironic structure glosses this mode of "consciousness" as follows: "The ironic language splits the subject into an empirical self that exists in a state of inauthenticity and a self that exists only in the form of a language that asserts the knowledge of this inauthenticity. This does not, however, make it into an authentic language, for to know inauthenticity is not the same as to be authentic."[64]

The first stanza of *Canzone* 23 provides a prologue to the narrative proper, and it is there that we find a presentation of the problematic of authenticity specific to this narrative. Immediately, in the course of the first six lines, we can discover two different plots, or perhaps two versions of the same plot. Reading according to the chronology of events as they might seem to have "happened," we learn that from an original state of innocence and liberty, the poet, through the agency of Love, has fallen into a state of fierce desire.

Nel dolce tempo de la prima etade,
che nascer vide et anchor quasi in herba
la fera voglia che per mio mal crebbe,
perchè cantando il duol si disacerba,
canterò com'io vissi in libertade,
mentre Amor nel mio albergo a sdegno s'ebbe.[65]

In the sweet time of my first age which saw born
and still almost unripe [or "green"] the fierce
desire which for my hurt grew—because, singing,
the pain is disembittered, I shall sing how I
lived in liberty while Love was scorned in my
abode. (translation mine) (23. 1–6)

The resolution to this painful situation would seem to be to
return to the original state of *libertade* which the *fera voglia*
has destroyed. The order of the appearance of the words, however, presents the *fera voglia* as possibly the prior of the two
states of being. This order would allow us to regard the term
libertade in a less innocent light. Line six itself, read literally,
qualifies the integrity and originality of the state of liberty by
the condition under which it has been maintained—*Amor . . .*
a sdegno s'ebbe. It remains to be shown only that Love's abey-
ance was a kind of false front concealing even from the poet
himself his status as a desiring being, and the prognosis for a
resolution becomes quite different. Clearly the poet cannot simply return to a self-mystifying condescension toward Love.
Nevertheless, *libertade,* in the sense of an absence or—what is
the same thing—fulfillment of desire, might still seem to be
the goal. For the state of desiring is represented not only as
painful, but as a state of non-being, or a non-state of being in
the sense that it raises certain questions concerning the status of
the self. One of the many questions we are left with by these
first six lines is whether the goal of liberty, ambiguous as it is,
is attainable. If the "original" state of freedom proves to be
illusory, how do we know there is an authentic version of freedom, and assuming that there were, how could it be distin-
guished from just another self-mystification? Might not the
pursuit of *libertade* turn out to be a nostalgic pursuit of that
first illusion after all?
    An even closer syntactical reading of these lines will dem-

onstrate the masking effect that the predications *vissi in libertade* and *mentre Amor nel mio albergo a sdegno s'ebbe* have on the subject "I" of this passage. The word order of this sequence of clauses is not the most "ordinary," with the result that there is, even syntactically, more than one way to read it. If by force of interpretive habit, we "returned" it to its "normal" order we could construe it approximately as follows: Because grief is disembittered by singing, I will sing of how I lived in liberty, while Love was held in disdain in my abode, during the sweet time of my first age which saw the birth and unripeness of the fierce desire that grew (into a laurel tree, we later learn) to my misfortune. Put this way, it looks as if the self "now" in grief knows the nature of his difference from the self "then" in liberty. He would know because he was there to witness the birth (the origin) and growth of his fierce desire. Because he (I) precedes this monstrous birth, he (the self) can be said to be something greater than and apart from that desire. It does not define him; he defines it. Or rather, by telling the story, he sets himself the task of defining desire (either by fulfilling it or denying it) as not constitutive of himself. The presumption of the narrating self is that he can discover the truth, that he can *know* what happened. This requires that he himself be complete or whole, as the desiring self, by definition a self which is wanting, is not. A slightly different way of describing the narrating self implied by this reading is to say that he stands outside the story, assuming a perspective apart from the perspective of any one point *in* the story. His outside position is necessary in order for the story not to be compromised by the temporality of its teller. If no outside position is posited, then it becomes impossible to determine whether change in the story is a function of the teller or of the tale.

The relationship of desire to temporality, the respective temporalities of the self who speaks or writes and the language which is spoken or written, is a central issue in *Canzone* 23's attempted narrative. If the self whose words we are reading is a desiring, incomplete self, then he cannot claim to stand outside of time. His perspective as a narrator is just as temporally limited as any of the perspectives he presents in his narrative. Time, instead of being seen as the medium through which the self is known and expressed, becomes simply a linear series of instants, precluding the possibility of any synthesis. If the desiring self were to claim to stand outside of time (and desire), the temporality of the language used to tell the story could be mistaken for that of events, and the shape of language be taken for the shape of history. An immediate example of this confusion of language and history is provided by the lines we are reading. The story told by the words rearranged in an order conventional *to sentences* bears a remarkable resemblance to the story told earlier when we thought we were putting events into their *historical* order. In both cases there is an original "I" from which there has been a falling away and to which there must be a return in order for the story to have an ending.

But through a careful manipulation of syntax, grammar, verb tense, and voice, the poet here also deconstructs this conflation, even if he does not escape from it. In the inverted form of the "sentence" which the poem presents, the "I," significantly, does not appear until the fourth line of the poem, after the birth and growth of desire and, again significantly, after it has presented the rationale that in singing, grief *si disacerba,* which we now notice may be read either passively— "is disembittered" (presumably by the singer)—or reflexively—"disembitters itself." The inverted *syntax* also points up the lack of *grammatical* dependence of the three clauses, *che nascer vide et anchor quasi in herba / la fera voglia, che per mio mal crebbe,* and *perché cantando il duol si disacerba,* on the subject of the sentence which is the first person singular pronoun implicit in *canterò.* The lack of any necessary relationship between this "I" and the first four lines of the poem, which describe the perspective of the present on the past, effectively deprives the "I" who will sing of any existence in the present (and because of the character of Italian verbs, the poet can suppress that "I" graphically as well) which might serve as a link between that future "I" and the "I" who lived, *io vissi,* in the past. Another clause which could be either passive or reflexive, *mentre Amor nel mio albergo a sdegno s'ebbe,* is similarly detached from the subject, and also from the *io* of the relative clause, as it would not be if Petrarch had exploited the possibility of using the *trapassato remoto,* or pluperfect—"I had lived"—instead of the *passato remoto* or simple past—"I lived"—in line five. Grammatically and syntactically, then, the sentence as it stands does not assume any connection even between the two conditions, *io vissi in libertade* and *mentre Amor nel mio albergo a sdegno s'ebbe* which are both of the past. Indeed all five *passato remoto* clauses are coequal, none is the cause or the effect of another, for just like the assumption of a link between past and future, the presentation of relationships among events in the past posits a self which knows itself in the present.

Technically speaking, though, we do not now have a sentence. If these clauses are not specified by the subject "I" then the sentence *qua* sentence is incoherent. It falls apart into a series of discontinuous clauses whose juxtaposition is suggestive, but whose relationship to each other cannot be established. At this point the confusion between history and language re-enters the picture in yet a different way, for it appears that the sort of self theoretically required to know history, to know what happened, may itself be seen as a linguistic category. It is sentence structure which requires a constitutive subject, an organizing principle which orients its other actions toward itself as their source and measure. The converse of the nonspecification of the clauses in the sentence at hand by the subject "I" is the nonspecification of the "I" by the predicate clauses, with the result that there is no way of knowing, as the poet later realizes, what "I" is or was—*Lasso, che son, che fui!* (Alas, what am I, what was I! [23. 30]). In other words, within language itself, as we have seen before in the contexts of other discussions, there is a kind of Ulyssean dissimulation. Subject and predicate are equally dependent upon each other, yet the subject is privileged as the organizing principle; its dependence is masked by the very elements it presumably governs. Action and agent are separated, the agent privileged over the action, in order for the sentence to "mean," but upon closer examination they become indistinguishable and the sentence collapses into circularity. The situation is exactly analogous to that of the self. When it posits itself as an absolute, atemporal being, it appears to have the capacity to mean something, to know itself, but when this being is unmasked, its meaning collapses into the continuum of temporality.

In the next eight lines, the inquiry into the relationship between language and self is extended to include, appropriately,

the relationship between the poem and the reader. Before looking at these lines as a unit, it is interesting to note that the last
three lines of the previous passage and the first three lines of
this one, themselves form a block that *does* claim for this *canzone* the status of an autobiographical account of the poet's love,
by saying that this story will be told as a straightforward chronological narrative:

> *perchè cantando il duol si disacerba,*
> *canterò com'io vissi in libertade,*
> *mentre Amor nel mio albergo a sdegno s'ebbe.*
> *Poi seguirò sì come a lui ne 'ncrebbe*
> *troppo altamente, e che di ciò m'avenne,*
> *di ch'io son facto a molta gente exempio:*

> because, singing, grief is disembittered, I shall
> sing how I lived in liberty while Love was scorned
> in my abode. Then I shall pursue how that chagrined
> him too deeply, and what happened to me on that
> account by which I have become an example for many
> people. (translation mine) (23. 4–9)

There is a story, the poet seems to say, but its articulations do
not fit the articulations of the language of the poem in which
it is told. It is to be set out as straightforwardly as possible, but
only a reader willing to accept an active role, to cross certain
boundaries and suspend certain beliefs and disbeliefs, will have
access to it.

The next "sentence" fairly aggressively demands such
readers:

> *Poi seguirò sì come a lui ne 'ncrebbe*
> *troppo altamente, e che di ciò m'avenne,*
> *di ch'io son facto a molta gente exempio:*
> *ben che 'l mio duro scempio*
> *sia scripto altrove, sì che mille penne*
> *ne son già stanche, et quasi in ogni valle*
> *rimbombi il suon de' miei gravi sospiri,*
> *ch'aquistan fede a la penosa vita.*

> Then I shall pursue how that chagrined him too
> deeply, and what happened to me on that account

by which I have become an example for many people:
although my hard ruin is written elsewhere so
that a thousand pens are already tired by it, and
almost every valley echoes to the sound of my
heavy sighs which obtain belief in my painful
life. (translation mine) (23. 7–14)

Here the syntax is strange, but not inverted. There is no more
"natural" order into which it could be rearranged in order to
make clearer the links among the events described. The confusion pointedly surrounds how the poet's earlier poems have
been received. It takes a moment to realize the *io son facto a
molta gente exempio* is not being qualified by *ben che 'l mio
duro scempio / sia scripto altrove,* that *ben che* refers all the
way back to *seguirò,* and that the clause which *ben che* introduces repeats in an expanded version the same information
summarized in line nine. The sentence does its work, on the
other hand, without the aid of a present and active "I" implied
or otherwise. In fact, this absence is the source of the repetitive-
ness of the sentence. The subject "I" is projected into the future, *seguirò,* and cannot yet integrate into a nonredundant
form the events of the past. Passive constructions abound—*che
di ciò m'avenne; io son facto; mio duro scempio / sia scripto*—
and pens become tired, valleys resound with the sound of the
poet's sighs, all without any agent being designated.

If by writing a sentence which does not dissimulate, the
poet confuses the reader, then the reader is implicated in the
confusion. But the poet's claim within the sentence that he has
been made an *exempio* and that his *gravi sospiri . . . aquistan
fede a la penosa vita* might be taken in a positive sense, meaning that reading this poetry has induced in readers an awareness
comparable to the poet's own. An *exemplum* is, after all, a story
in which other people may see themselves and through which
they may discover themselves. The religious overtones of *exempio, fede,* and *penosa* (which means both painful and repentant
and which may include a pun on pen/writing) lends the
achievement of such self-consciousness the air of a conversion,
though a highly unorthodox one. Instead of leading to the
definition of self, this conversion to the poem precipitates a
kind of identity crisis.

The last six lines of the stanza retrospectively highlight some of the details of the situation that has just been described, and serve as both apology and warning to the reader who might continue unselfconsciously to try to follow the poem's narrative line. First they state the obvious. That is, that the retrospective structure of memory, the grammar and syntax in terms of which the past might be apprehended, is not operative here. If subject and predicate, predicate and predicate, all turn out to be the same, if the "I" of the poem is or has only "one thought," then the kind of figurative reading that would make of this "I" a self with a memory must, as the poem says, be forgotten. Selves and memories are themselves figures which can be constituted and "read" only if there are differences—between moments in the past, between past and present—and continua maintaining these differences in some kind of relation. Here, difference is reduced to sameness while continuity is replaced by disjunction:

> E se qui la memoria non m'aita
> come suol fare, iscusilla i martiri
> et un penser che solo angoscia dalle,
> tal ch' ad ogni altro fa voltar le spalle,
> e mi face obliar me stesso a forza:
> ché tèn di me quel d'entro, et io la scorza.

> And here if memory does not help me as it is wont to
> do, let the martyrdoms excuse it and one thought which
> gives it only anguish, so that it [the thought] makes
> me turn my back on every other [thought] and makes me
> forget myself by necessity, for it [the thought] holds
> what is within me, and I the bark. (translation mine)
> (23. 15–20)

The term la memoria immediately refocuses attention as well on the references to writing in the preceding passage—scritto; sì che mille penne ne son già stanche; and the possible pun in la penosa vita. If it is not an event in the poet's past and its relationship to the present that the poem is trying to unfold, but rather, as I have suggested, a different way of writing "history," then this written or penned life, and particularly the subject pronoun "I" which so powerfully evokes both the grammar of selfhood and the syntax of memory, present something of an obstacle. Not only does memory not help, it is a positive hindrance.[66]

What is called for and what is up to a point attempted is a mode of writing and reading that at once confounds "memory" and tries to institute a new interpretive structure. For "writing" not to be confused with "memory," though, is practically impossible. Somehow signs which remain the same as before must signify differently than before, yet already as I write this description, even the before/after distinction threatens to reinscribe the new structure within the old. This problem gains particular pertinence as the question of the fate of the self as subject is raised. The self, whether conceived of as subject pronoun or as conscious human being—it makes no difference for the moment whether we are talking about sentences or life histories—keeps getting in the way, misleading the narrative, and yet the fact that the "I" blocks and distorts the narrative is the prime indicator that there is something wrong in the narrative mode itself. The subject "I" finds itself in the untenable position of having to claim a privileged position for itself, an autonomous or ahistorical perspective from which to identify an historically significant moment (a moment when historical thinking is or ought to be changing) at the same time that the moment of (or decision to) change denies the possibility of such an ahistorical perspective. In order to tell the story he wants to tell, the poet must commit the error of universalizing even as his narrative shows this universalizing self to be an illusion. In other words, exactly as he says, in order to prevent the poetry from being reabsorbed in the figural mode from which it is trying to emerge, the poet risks losing—sacrificing or "martyring"—the self in terms of both language and history.

The relation of the self to language and history becomes at best irreducibly ambiguous, for though he loses a self, the poet possibly gains a sign. *La scorza* in line twenty does not mean "the body" as most glosses would have it, but, as is clearly stated, the *io*, the narrating subject.[67] Similarly *di me quel d'entro* is not the soul, but the object of narration which has been "taken away." The Augustinian doctrine of letter and spirit which lies behind the commentators' partial mistake *is* being invoked here: the bark or skin—the written "I"—corresponding to the "letter" and the *quel dentro di me* corresponding to the "spirit." In contrast to Augustine's letter which is literal and historical, though, Petrarch's is ahistorical and fictional. Analogously, Augustine's eschatological spirit is supplanted by Petrarch's literal, historical pith or content. If the semiotics of this kind of sign could be worked out, then it might appear that through the sign the absent self might be recuperated. Through observing, as we have done, the *performance* of the fictional "I," it might seem that in some sense we have come to "know" the situation of a self. Petrarch's performative discourse (however passive, absent, indeed, *un*performative it has been shown to be) attempts to present an alternative to figurative discourse and the concept of history it implies.

The problem with Petrarch's performative rhetoric here is that it may work *only* vis à vis a figurative structure. Figurative and performative modes of discourse are, or threaten to remain, reciprocally defining images of each other.[68] Rather than reflecting a self, however indirectly, the performative "I" can be shown to be simply a mutually mirrored image of its figurative counterpart. This is a problem that remains at the end of the first stanza and, as I have shown, at the end of the poem. If "I" is not to be read figuratively but performatively, does it then become the first of a series of signs in a new performative mode of discourse? Or does it remain so inevitably tied to its figurative "source" that no such emancipation is possible? The text, by itself, cannot claim the former, and, as we have seen, deconstructs the latter figurative reading that might be imposed upon it. There remains, in addition, a third possibility—that of exploring the poetic moment itself, as it belongs to neither one mode of discourse nor the other, but to both.

In a passage from the Narcissus story in Ovid's *Metamorphoses,* Narcissus describes in narrative form the duplication of his own gestures in what he does not yet know to be his reflection:

> *spem mihi nescio quam vultu promittis amico,*
> *cumque ego porrexi tibi bracchia, porrigis ultro,*
> *cum risi, adrides; lacrimas quoque saepe notavi*
> *me lacrimante tuas; nutu quoque signa remittis*
> *et, quantum motu formosi suspicor oris,*
> *verba refers aures non pervenientia nostras!*

You offer some hope with your friendly expression,
and when I have outstretched my arms to you, you out-
stretch on the other side, when I have smiled, you
smile back; you give back signs to my nod, and, as
I suspect from the motion of your beautiful lips,
you return words that are not reaching my ears![69]
(*Met.* III, 457–62)

As he moves, smiles, and greets, Narcissus interprets the simultaneous gestures he makes and sees reflected as a sequence of
invitations and answers. The result of his narrative interpretation is his recognition that the "history" of his love affair is a
distorted image of a certain relationship to his own image—
iste ego sum: sensi, nec me mea fallit imago (Oh, I am he! I
have felt it, I know now my own image [*l.* 463]).[70] What
Narcissus does next is very interesting. Neither the narrative
image nor the non-narrative situation (the mirror image interpreted non-narratively) is very illuminating in and of itself.
But these two images, which are themselves mirror images of
each other (the mirror image instigates the narrative, the narrative leads to the understanding that the mirror image is an
imago and not an other), are then compared or combined to
form a composite picture of a self which constitutes and is constituted by both images:

> *uror amore mei: flammas moveoque feroque.*
>
> . . . .
>
> *quod cupio mecum est: inopem me copia fecit.*
>
> . . . .
>
> *nec mihi mors gravis est posituro morte dolores,*
> *hic, qui diligitur, vellem diuturnior esset;*
> *nunc duo concordes anima moriemur in una.*

> I burn with love of myself: I both kindle and
> suffer the flames. . . . What I desire, I have:
> plenty makes me poor. . . . Death is not threaten-
> ing to me for in death I shall leave my griefs,
> I would that he, who is loved, might live longer;
> now we two shall die together in one breath.
> (*ll.* 464, 466, 471–73)

The "I" is problematized, the "voice" of Narcissus becomes a poetic rather than a historical voice, as the disappearance of his body and its replacement by a flower, after his death, signify. And, no less significantly, Narcissus does not die the violent death of so many of the protagonists in the stories surrounding this one in Book III—"characters" who never realize or realize too late (as I shall explain in a moment) the insubstantiality of their "historical" identities.

Just before the *congedo* of *Canzone* 23 the poet represents himself as threatened by the fate of Actaeon, one of the Ovidian characters whose stories precede that of Narcissus in Book III:

> . . . *i' senti' trarmi de la propria imago*
> *et in un cervo solitario et vago*
> *di selva in selva ratto mi trasformo,*
> *et anchor de' miei can fuggo lo stormo.*

> I felt myself drawn from my own image
> and into a solitary wandering stag from wood
> to wood quickly I am transformed and still
> I flee the belling of my hounds. (23. 158–60)

The intervening stanzas of the poem, nevertheless, operate similarly to Narcissus' "self-conscious" discourse. The metamorphoses, each involving what seems to be an interaction between the poet and his "powerful lady," are presented narratively, sequentially, but each incident may also be understood as analogous to and in some way simultaneous with the others. If by the beginning of the second stanza, which will serve as our example, it is clear that "I" is a fiction, the question then becomes, what images, narrative and non-narrative, does this fiction generate? How is the fiction itself altered in the course of comparing and contrasting these images? And how do they in turn change with these alterations? We find that much of what can be deduced from the first stanza here becomes explicit. The first nine lines offer a more "faithful" account of the nature or state of the self unresponsive to Love than that given (thematically) in the first stanza:

> *I' dico che dal dì che 'l primo assalto*
> *mi diede Amor, molt' anni eran passati,*
> *sì ch'io cangiava il giovenil aspetto;*

e dintorno al mio cor pensier' gelati
facto avean quasi adamantino smalto
ch'allentar non lassava il duro affetto.
Lagrima anchor non mi bagnava il petto
né rompea il sonno, e quel che in me non era,
mi pareva un miracolo in altrui.

I say that since the day when Love gave me the
first assault many years had passed, so that
I was changing my youthful aspect; and around my
heart frozen thoughts had made almost an adaman-
tine enamel such that it did not allow my hard
suffering to loosen. Not a tear yet bathed my
breast or broke my sleep, and that which was
not in me seemed a miracle in others. (23. 21–29)

The realization that what before was called *libertade* should
now be described as hardness of heart follows from the recognition that the "I" who writes is a simulacrum exactly coincident with the *primo assalto* of Love. It is he (it) that speaks as
of that day (*I' dico che dal dì che*), and over the course of time
this simulacrum has "hardened" or literalized itself. We have
just caught it in the first stanza thinking of itself as "real" and
hence "free," although it also spoke of its *duro scempio* or hard
ruin which is merely the reification of incompleteness. The
miraculous thing is that others should not suffer this delusion
(*il duro affetto*), but rather the tears and sleeplessness of a
more conscious self-alienation (perhaps, though, a function of
a figural self-reading). It should be noticed that these lines are
very circumspect about the role of Love in the creation of this
self. No causal link is insisted upon between the aging, changing, and hardening of heart of the protagonist and the *primo
assalto*. The lines beginning *e dintorno al mio cor pensier'
gelati* (*l.* 24) are grammatically parallel either to *io cangiava il
giovenil aspetto* (*l.* 23) (both clauses modifying *molt'anni
eran passati*) or, more directly, to *molt'anni eran passati*. In
either case, the years would have passed regardless of Love's
intervention. The wary poet is equally circumspect about claim-
ing any causal role for himself. With the passing years *he* has
changed, either his looks or his point of view or both, but for
the rest he portrays himself as the object of impersonal forces

and situations—*assalto / mi diede; pensier' gelati / facto avean; Lagrima anchor non mi bagnava; quel che in me non era / mi pareva* (emphases mine).

One conclusion to be inferred from the symmetrical roles of Love and "I" in the narrative unfolding of these nine lines is that the play between them is shadow play. As one goes, so goes the other. The hypostatization of the self, and the constitution of the aspect of the self which would prevent hypostatization as if this aspect were itself a figure or force, are two sides of the same imaginative act. The reader here can "reduce" Love from the status of an independent and dominant figurative presence to that of a mote in the eye of the narrator, and thus reduce the narrator, too, to the status of an illusion. Such a reduction is available to the narrator whose drama we are following, and seems, in fact, to be his reading as well. *Lasso che son? che fui?* (*l.* 30). This reading is both rigorous and appropriate; its only disadvantage is that it stops the narrative in its tracks. *Without* Love, without the hypostatization, there is no narrator. Abruptly what has been recounted as a situation in the past overwhelms the present. The "I" now is in the same boat as the "I" in the past about which he was telling. The rest of this stanza is, appropriately, devoted to the lover's metamorphosis into the laurel, the figure through which the subsequent narrative becomes possible—and escape from the narrative problematic impossible.[71]

To conclude this discussion of the problem of history and language as it is confronted in *Canzone* 23, I would again survey an aspect of the *Commedia,* this time to arrive at a triangulation of Dante, Petrarch, and Ovid on the Narcissistic situation of narrative. One of the richest imagistic veins in the *Commedia* is the figurative manipulation of glass, mirrors, and reflected light. The bottom of *Inferno* consists of the frozen lake of Cocytus strewn with shades, completely covered by the ice, who show through *come festuca in vetro* (like straw in glass [*Inf.* XXXIV, 12]). As Satan, stuck in the middle of this frozen lake, turns out to be a grotesque parody of the holy Trinity, so these worst of mortal sinners, the treacherous to lords and benefactors, are reduced to imperfections, insignificant flaws in a glass which nevertheless, as a whole, mirrors God's will. The sinners throughout *Inferno,* as this imagery confirms, have been part of a legible discourse, even if pilgrim, guide, and reader have not always known how to read it. With the reversal of right and left, and up and down, which occurs when Vergil takes Dante on his back to climb down to Satan's crotch and then up his flanks into the southern hemisphere, with Dante's conversion, it is understood that the region left behind has been a region of three-dimensional mirror writing. The material of this mirror may have been coarse and distorting, but the chief problem of legibility has been the pilgrim's own inappropriate orientation.

If one takes the name Dante as an example, and tries to read it from left to right as it appears in a two-dimensional mirror, one gets some idea of the problems posed by Infernal writing. Of the five letters in

ƎTИAᗡ

two, the T and the A, because of their bilateral symmetry, seem perfectly clear. Nevertheless, their relationship to each other is the reverse of what it should be if we are to understand DANTE from these letters. Of the other three, two more, the E and the D may be recognizable as letters, but the letters themselves are backwards—just as is the order in which they occur. The N is possibly the most difficult to recognize as a letter, and unless all the markings are understood to be letters, there is no reason to assume that together they constitute a word, a unit of meaning of a different order than that of the letters that make it up. Further problems are presented in *Inferno* by the absence of light. The sinners themselves, the impurities of the glass, reflect next to nothing of God's truth, and it is *Inferno* as a whole which serves as the mirror

WORD or ᗡЯOW

dimly and cryptically reflecting divine light.

In *Purgatorio,* where souls do penance, where they refine away the remaining husks or straws of sin and error in order to make themselves worthy of heaven, the glass is always molten, as it is when Dante says he would have plunged into molten glass to cool himself when he had to pass through the fire in order to enter the earthly paradise (*Purg.* XXVII, 49). The souls here are not yet perfect reflectors of truth, but they are being formed into mirrors just as molten glass might be. One can see why *Purgatorio* is the most difficult canticle to read, for, though the pilgrim's vision has been righted, the material with which he must deal is in constant flux. Presumably the mirrors into which the Purgatorial shades and Dante himself are being transformed will reverse the negative mirror image of the truth found in *Inferno* into a positive likeness, but in the meantime the reader must prepare himself to interpret his observations in either way or even both ways, continually readjusting his focus and interpretive direction to suit the conditions of each particular situation in the transformational process.

The mirror imagery of *Paradiso,* in all its dazzling detail, is beyond the scope of my description here, but two instances of the pilgrim's response to *Paradiso*'s mirror-like inhabitants pertain to Petrarch's and Dante's respective understandings of the Narcissistic situation. In *Paradiso* III, Dante's first encounter with heavenly spirits in the sphere of the moon, he rightly takes them for mirror images, but mistakenly thinks he should look away from them for that reason:

> *Quali per vetri trasparenti e tersi,*
>   *o ver per acque nitide e tranquille,*
>   *non sì profonde che i fondi sien persi,*
> *tornan d'i nostri visi le postille*
>   *debili sì, che perla in bianca fronte*
>   *non vien men forte a le nostre pupille;*
> *tali vid' io più facce a parlar pronte;*
>   *per ch'io dentro a l'error contrario corsi*
>   *a quel ch'accese amor tra l'omo e 'l fonte.*

> As through smooth and transparent glass, or through
> clear and tranquil waters, yet not so deep that the
> bottom be lost, the outlines of our faces return so
> faint that a pearl on a white brow comes not less
> boldly to our eyes, so did I behold many a coun-
> tenance eager to speak; wherefore I fell into the
> contrary error to that which kindled love between
> the man and the fountain. (*Par.* III, 10–18)

The pilgrim reacts according to reflexes developed in *Inferno* to avoid Narcissus' "error" of taking the mirror image for reality or truth. Mirrors in heaven, though, have the effect of undoing the kind of error met with in *Inferno*. Putting aside the question of the source of divine writing, we see that *Inferno* and *Paradiso* are like two mirrors facing each other, the second one setting right the letters and words reflected in the first, so that in this reflection of a reflection we may read the "original" text. For now that text *must* be read as it appears in the second mirror, for the ultimate reality it represents far surpasses the pilgrim's or our capacity to see and understand.

Nevertheless, there are risks involved in trying to read even this fair copy. In Canto XVIII the pilgrim must be reprimanded by Beatrice for forgetting the dangers of Narcissistic reflection. In the preceding canto, which we have already had several occasions to consider in connection with Dante's poetics, Cacciaguida has glossed the dark prophecies for Dante's future received from various figures in *Inferno*, urging Dante nevertheless to write the poem that will turn the great and powerful against him. Canto XVIII opens:

> Già si godeva solo del suo verbo
> quello specchio beato, e io gustava
> lo mio, temprando col dolce l'acerbo;
> e quella donna ch'a Dio mi menava
> disse: "Muta pensier; pensa ch'i' sono
> presso a colui ch'ogni torto disgrava."

Already that blessed mirror was enjoying only its
own thoughts, and I was tasting mine, tempering the
bitter with the sweet, when the lady who was leading me to God said, "Change your thought: consider
that I am in His presence who lightens the burden
of every wrong." (*Par.* XVIII, 1–6)

Pondering his future exile, Dante at first fails to see that this exile actually confirms the "nourishing" truth that he is to write about in his poem. The prophecies of his exile, legacies from *Inferno*, operate here something like the letters T and A in the

DANTE / ƎTИAⅮ

example I used earlier. At first glance they look the same whether they are read forward or backward, but the similarity is deceptive. When Dante thinks he has just heard the same thing from Cacciaguida that he heard in *Inferno,* he responds in the same way he responded the first time, reading his fate under the aspect of pain and bitterness. In other words, he reads A and T as if they came from the ominously knotty hieroglyphic ƎTИAD instead of the reassuringly straightforward DANTE. Beatrice immediately commands him to look into the mirrors of her eyes in order to dispel this error before Cacciaguida resumes with an explication of the souls who appear in the sphere of Mars.

What the pilgrim does here is to short-circuit the effect that the second mirror is supposed to have. Like Narcissus, who fails at first to see that the image to which he grows attached is in part a function of the medium which seems to bar his way to grasping that illusory other—and as he consequently misunder stands the image to be an entity in isolation from and at odds with the reflecting pool—so Dante, by getting the sense of the words of Cacciaguida that pertain to his earthly destiny one hundred and eighty degrees wrong, suffers a misunderstanding which, if uncorrected, would threaten the integrity of Cacciaguida's larger meaning.

It is not my purpose here to give as well a reading of Ovid's Narcissus, but a reading of Dante's and Petrarch's readings of Ovid necessarily entails making some general statements about that story.[72] Ovid's Narcissus, Tiresias divined, would have lived to a "well-ripened age" (*tempora maturae*) if he had never "known" himself. That is, if he had never been tempted by his reflection to conceive of either an other or himself as a discrete entity, a "knowable" subject, he would not have become enamored of the illusion of that state and wasted away in its thrall. His eventual recognition of his reflection, not as a discrete entity to be appropriated, but as an image of his own status as one intersection in the fluid web of changes and exchanges which make up the Ovidian world, does not succeed in rescuing him from his deadly enamorment. In the stories surrounding that of Narcissus, other characters, too, deliberately and undeliberately, behave in a manner that threatens to disrupt the ebb and flow of the Ovidian world—"scoffing at the gods" (Pentheus) or simply "seeming" a happy ruler (Cadmus, the grandfather of Actaeon and the founder of Thebes). Paradoxically it is their apparent authority or position that, in fact, most closely approximates death or stoppage in terms of the universe of which they are a part. Narcissus' disappearance is actually one of the least horrible "ends" in Book III, perhaps because Narcissus is said to realize the futility of his attachment to the insubstantial image of his (or another's) substantiality before he dies. The fact that he, in some sense, wills his own premature "death" by remaining enamored of the image is what makes him for Dante the type of the "unripe" (*acerbo*) sinner. But for Ovid, Narcissus' awareness, as opposed to the fatal ignorance of Actaeon and the disbelief of Pentheus, seems to soften the shock of physically discovering or experiencing the lie of the Narcissistic self's substance and integrity.

Ovid's Narcissus grasps the significance, if not the moral imperative deduced therefrom by Dante, of the simultaneity of subject and reflection. *Inopem me copia fecit* (Plenty makes me poor [*l.* 466]), he laments when he discovers that what he desires he at the same time has or is or "makes." Because the subject and its reflection are *in*separable, they must be regarded as the same: either equally illusory, and therefore, for Dante, equally inappropriate as objects of desire; or equally desirable for the intimations of autonomy and sovereignty, being and knowing that both the notion of the subject, and its concomitant capacity to be present or almost present to itself, have to offer. There is, for Dante, the third possibility, performed in the play of images between *Inferno* and *Paradiso,* that a thorough investigation of the constitutive relationship itself might be a means of freeing desire, and hence knowledge, from their bondage to the illusory subject. But for Ovid Narcissus' consciousness of the self's insubstantiality, and consequently of the baselessness of its desiring and knowing, is the only "knowledge" available.

Dante's revision of Ovid on this score is a principal element in his difference from Petrarch, who, as we have seen, renews the Ovidian problematic, especially in *Canzone* 23. The poem ends with the poet assuming exactly the same position as Narcissus:

né per nova figura il primo alloro
seppi lassar ché pur la sua dolce ombra
ogni men bel piacer del cor mi sgombra.

Nor for a new figure have I known how to leave
the first laurel, for still its sweet shade clears
away from my heart any less beautiful pleasure.
(translation mine) (23. 167–69)

The shadow of the laurel is his shadow and he is, in some sense, its shadow (*Ne per nova figura il primo alloro / seppi lassar* [*ll.* 167–68]), but his awareness of that fact prevents his reification of himself in the image of some seemingly more substantial counter. With this statement the issue of narrative in the *Canzoniere* is definitively closed. The "history" of this "self" cannot be told as a story, except as a "story" of its nonnarrative structure, a structure which will always need a narrative leading to its (and the "narrative's") discovery or unmasking. This story is the story of reading the *Canzoniere*—not unlike the Ovidian "reading" of Narcissus, and akin to Dante's "double-play" of reflecting images. The significant (signifying) difference, as I have been suggesting, would be that where Dante's "reading" is located as a moral imperative for the pilgrim confronted with the text's presentations, or for the reader facing the representation(s) which is the text of the *Commedia,* Petrarch's "reading" is a critical-linguistic investigation invested and inscribed in the *Canzoniere* and its language themselves.

III
Negative Stylistics:
A Reading of
Petrarch's *Trionfi*

Metaphor creates a new
reality from which
the original appears to
be unreal.
Wallace Stevens, "Adagia"

If *Canzone* 23 identifies a moment or situation in which narrative becomes extremely problematic as a poetic possibility, the *Trionfi*, I would argue, takes on the ambitious project of attempting to create a new poetics of narration. Though a much less successful work than the *Canzoniere*, it departs even more radically from a figural mode of reading and writing, being a relatively continuous narrative (though probably written over the course of more than thirty years of Petrarch's life) in which significance is not recuperative. It is a poem which actively discourages the attempt to discern figural or allegorical significance in either its own substance or its (frequently literary historical) subject matter. In proposing the reading of the *Trionfi* which follows, then, I intend to round out my discussion of the poetics of Petrarch's Italian poetry—to further substantiate the claims I have made in the first chapter concerning the ways in which Petrarch's concept of history and his poetics implicate each other, and to extend my argument that Petrarch intends his (and others') texts to be read relationally rather than figuratively. I would also suggest how literary history serves the present in retrieving this "unreadable" text of the past. The *Trionfi* seems to have backfired in its attempt wholly to subvert certain structures of interpretation, not unlike several more recent texts which, it now appears, have also stimulated the very readings which their rhetoric most deeply challenges. Reading the *Trionfi* allegorically or figuratively, as most commentators have done, is like searching for "plot" and "character" in *Finnegans Wake,* like trying to determine the "authenticity" of Rousseau's *Confessions.* In coming to terms with a text which has been misread so thoroughly and which is now mostly unread (though for several centuries the *Trionfi* was more popular than either the *Commedia* or the *Canzoniere,* it now has little appeal, and is usually regarded as "bad" poetry), it becomes necessary to acknowledge two sets of conceptual boundaries, those against which Petrarch's poetry sets itself and those which separate the sensibilities of one time from those of another. The effort to see and understand what Petrarch is doing in the *Trionfi,* therefore, might serve to reintroduce history into our contemporary discussions of "meaning." It would appear at once that present-day theories of discourse are not alone in trying to disassociate meaning from notions of representation, identity, truth, and unity; and that trying to make this break has not always "meant" the same thing.

Our sense of how the *Trionfi* was received in the fifteenth and sixteenth centuries comes from two major sources, notable for their parallel development: written commentaries and pictorial representations. From 1475, when the first extant and universally influential commentary of the poem appeared, until at least 1582, the literary world seems readily to have accepted the *Trionfi* as a moralizing, allegorical representation of the growth and progress of the soul of Everyman as exemplified by the speaker in the poem who was, in turn, taken to be Petrarch.[1] The seminal allegorical gloss of Bernardo da Pietro Lapini da Montalcino, known as Illicino, was echoed by virtually every other Italian commentator for a century and paraphrased as well by Spanish, Portuguese, and German translators. In his 1582 edition with commentary of Petrarch's Italian poetry, Castelvetro presented a fresh and somewhat closer reading of the poem, but he still identified the *Trionfi* thematically as an account of the poet's repentance and conversion. At the close of the century, on the other hand, at the height of the theoretical debate over the epic genre, it seemed to the theoretician Tomaso Costa that the *Trionfi*'s diction, rhetoric, metaphors—*Quella purità e proprietà di lingua, quell' armonia, quella gravità . . .*—were evidence that the work was intended to be an epic.[2]

Pictorial representations of the *Trionfi,* which number in the thousands, evolved along a similar course. Fifteenth- and sixteenth-century pictorial triumphs depict symmetrical series of allegorical figures, seated on chariots drawn by symbolically appropriate beasts, surrounded by groups of captives and attendants. As artists as well as writers of the sixteenth century were drawn to the heroic, the triumphal motif becomes more classically drawn, the groups of captives and attendants more heroically full of literary and historical characters. But with these stylistic changes, the series becomes more rather than less continuous and unified. The iconography of these paintings, frescoes, medals, miniatures, birth trays, *cassoni* or chests, and tapestries is at once so standardized and so discrepant from the poem itself that the puzzle of Renaissance illustrations of the *Trionfi* has become a major art historical preoccupation.[3] Since the earliest paintings predate Illicino, art historians have thought that perhaps an allegorizing commentary, now lost, was written between the first appearance of the poem and its first pictorial representation. This hypothesis, of course, merely begs our question. Whichever came first, an allegorizing written commentary or an allegorizing painted commentary, the fact remains that both commentators and artists, and presumably their publics, appear to have responded to the poem as if it presented a model of allegorical and visionary coherence. Indeed, the device or motif of the triumph, first made available by Petrarch, remained enormously popular as a vehicle for the presentation of ideas and ideals for three centuries after he wrote.

The *Trionfi* itself, I would maintain, is a radically antiallegorical, nonvisionary poem; the triumph motif, as Petrarch uses it, is a literary construct chosen to call attention to the fictive nature of both the dream vision and the dreamer who dreams it. The two most obvious sources of the motif already suggest as much. The *Commedia* is once again close to the surface of Petrarch's writing, a relationship underscored in the *Trionfi* by its appropriation of *terza rima* as well as by its all-pervasive verbal and thematic echoes of Dante's poem. The work bears a specific resemblance to the pageant of Beatrice and the Church Militant in the last four cantos of *Purgatorio*. Significantly, Dante's elaborate, highly stylized triumph calls attention to itself as spectacle *as opposed to* event. It represents a departure from the narrative mode in which it is embedded, substituting artifice for event, presumably because at this point the distinction between letter and spirit, between the literal and the figural, begins to break down. It serves as a bridge to the poetics of *Paradiso* where Dante largely abandons narrative, where the "literal" reality with which the pilgrim is confronted remains by definition out of reach of mortal minds, where all the poetry is "equally" metaphorical. A brief evocation by John Freccero of the poetics of *Paradiso* is relevant, by contrast, to the direction taken by Petrarch in the *Trionfi:* "It is in difference that meaning is born, like the difference between two phonetic sounds, unintelligible in themselves, yet constituting meaning when linked together. So with the poem, which manages to approach its conclusion and silence by the gradual dissipation of all difference between light and light, and yet remains as the shadow of all that the experience is not, as irreducibly literary as 'a pearl upon a milk white brow.' "[4] Petrarch, in adopting the atypical mode of the Dantesque triumph for his *entire* poem, seems to indicate that even ordinary events, images, and realities are somehow "out of reach." History is indecipherable, and the beautiful fictions of poets remain the only source of pattern and coherence, though they are no longer allegories of anything but themselves. Difference, as we shall see shortly, is irreducibly literary in the *Trionfi,* but gradually exaggerated, not dissipated. The meanings which would be born of different elements rhetorically associated by such means as spatial contiguity, synecdochal representation, exemplification, etc., become unintelligible as the poem renounces the rhetorical means by which such linkages are made, and approaches its own particular version of completion and silence.

The other clearly recognizable model of the Petrarchan motif is the Roman military triumph, descriptions of which Petrarch had read in Roman histories as well as in medieval compilations.[5] But, as Petrarch's countless remarks in letters, meditations, other poems, and the *Trionfi* itself indicate, he conceived of the Roman civilization whose glory was embodied in the triumph as definitively past, as absent from the present. As I noted in my opening chapter, he warned that Rome was an empty name; the reality to which it once pointed, though superior to his own degenerate society, was lost. *Non far idolo un nome / Vano senza soggetto.*[6] In the *Trionfi* the speaker portrays himself as deeply enamored of idols, images, and empty names, but none of them, finally, takes precedence over another. Instead they work against each other or cancel each other out, depriving their succession of metaphorical or paradigmatic coherence. No total picture or global view of life ever emerges, while the fluidity and instability of the categories in terms of which such views might be constructed are insisted upon.

The *Trionfi*'s own characteristic narrative strategy is all the more conspicuous for its avoidance of any transcendent design, once the fictive status of the poem's thematic contents has been suggested. The attraction that a succession of apparently autonomous, if radically fictive, performances holds for the poem's protagonist gives the poem its chief means of forwarding the plot, such as there is a plot. At the beginning of the poem, for example, the speaker recounts how, when he sank into sleep in a *chiuso loco* or enclosed place, on an anniversary of his first falling in love, a burst of light ushered in a scene of pomp and circumstance which transported him not only out of his own state of mind, but out of the lackluster reality of his century. The vision of a great lord, *com' un di color che 'n Campidoglio / trionfal carro a gran gloria conduce* (like one of those which the triumphal chariot bore to great glory on the Capital [TC I, 14–15]), promises a new field of vision, perhaps even an alternative to an intractable reality:

> *I' che gioir di tal vista non soglio*
> *per lo secol noioso in ch' i' mi trovo,*
> *voto d' ogni valor, pien d' ogni orgoglio,*
> *   l' abito in vista sì leggiadro e novo*
> *mirai, alzando gli occhi gravi e stanchi*
> *ch'altro diletto che 'mparar non provo.*

Unused to rejoicing in such a sight, because of the
tiresome century in which I live, devoid of valor,
full of pride, I looked upon this delightful, aston-
ishing sight, and, raising my tired and heavy eyes,
I feel no other inclination than to learn about it.[7]
(TC I, 16–21)

This is only the first of many occasions upon which the poet is completely removed out of one scene into another without displaying any capacity or inclination to integrate them con-

ceptually. On another occasion the dramatic possibilities of conflict and tension not only go undeveloped, but are actively
dissolved and dispersed by the poem's refusal to remain within
any one framework long enough for these tensions to build.
After Massinissa, a figure encountered in the second *capitolo* of
the *"Triumphus cupidinis,"* finishes recounting the story of the
conflict between his love for the Carthaginian queen Sophonisba
and his duty to the Roman Empire, a story which Petrarch had
told elsewhere, in his Latin epic the *Africa,* and which here
causes the poet-dreamer to dissolve in pity, Sophonisba herself
abruptly enters the conversation to announce that she still does
not like Italians. Much to the amusement of Massinissa, she and
the poet-dreamer thereupon begin arguing about politics, and
the melancholy mood is broken. Sophonisba has the last word:
*s'Africa pianse, Italia non ne rise: / demandatene pur l' istorie
vostre* (if Africa weeps, Italy does not smile on account of it:
just look in your own histories [TC II, 83–84]), and Massinissa
smiles at the point scored against his own homeland. History,
suddenly, stretches out beyond the end of the story of Sophonisba's death which becomes only a minor incident in a tem-
porary reversal.

Such freedom, the fluidity of history's shape, the ease with
which political and personal lines are drawn and redrawn, can
be exhilarating, but it can also begin to look like too much of a
good thing. The most striking example of the poem's antidra-
matics is the reappearance of Laura, declaring her complete re-
ciprocation of the poet's feeling for her, in a dream he has after
witnessing her death in the *"Triumphus mortis."* Once again
the poetic effect is achieved by getting beyond endings, the most
definitive of which would seem to be death. Laura rises up from
beyond the veil of misapprehensions, dreads, and fears which
oppress the "living" to dispel the errors of her deluded lover:

> *"Viva son io e tu se' morto ancora,"*
> *diss' ella, "e sarai sempre infin che giunga*
> *per levarti di terra l' ultima ora."*

"I am alive and you are still dead," she said,
"and so you will be until the final hour arrives
to lift you from the earth." (TM II, 22–24)

His greatest misapprehension has been, of course, that she did not love him. In creating this impression, he is told, she has been a benevolent and successful manipulator of appearances. She explains:

> *Mai diviso*
> *da te non fu 'l mio cor, né già mai fia;*
> *ma temprai la tua fiamma col mio viso.*

> Never has my heart been divided from you, nor
> will it ever be; but I tempered your flame with
> my face. (TM II, 88–90)

Now, it seems, her past behavior can finally be demystified:

> *Questi fur teco miei ingegni e mie arti:·*
> *or benigne accoglienze ed ora sdegni;*
> *tu 'l sai che n' ai cantato in molte parti.*

> These were my arts and stratagems with you:
> now gentle welcome and now disdain; you know
> this who have sung of it in many places. (TM II, 109–11)

This explanation or new interpretation of Laura's gestures and expressions while on earth, though, is as suspect as the easy pieties with which the dream-Laura opens the exchange. What proof is there that this dream within a dream has any substance to it, that it is not simply the product of the dreamer's own distressed imagination? In an odd turn, the poet-dreamer tearfully confesses his own difficulty in believing her and her words, despite his desire to do so. His doubt elicits sixteen *terzine* of attempts on the part of the phantom Laura to prove, by recalling and analyzing various of their past encounters, that she means what she says, that this vision is trustworthy. We may feel that she protests too much, but her lover's response is somewhat different. However questionable or fleeting his moment of retrospective illumination may be, the imposition of "meaning" or "meaningfulness" on what had previously been at best an ambiguous situation succeeds in soothing and relieving him:

> *"Quant 'io soffersi mai, soave e leve,"*
> *dissi, "m' ha fatto il parlar dolce e pio."*

"However much I have ever suffered," I said,
"your sweet and pious words have made me calm
and happy." (TM II, 184–85)

The opposite conclusion remains to be inferred from the
way this episode is *written*. We have just learned, the storyteller
herself has just explained, how easily the arts of expression can
be manipulated and used to manipulate. We then observe the
poet-dreamer succumb to precisely this sort of manipulation.
Neither his response nor the ambiguous status of the dream-
within-a-dream establishes the authority of the phantom Laura's
version of the relationship over the earlier version enacted in
the Triumphs of Love and Chastity. Rather than a vertical hierarchy of interpretations approaching closer and closer to the
truth, we find a horizontal succession of situations operating
such that whatever is most immediate seems most authoritative,
or at least most compelling, to the dreamer. Petrarch's wording
and the positioning of his words are very careful here—*"Quant'
io soffersi mai, soave e leve," / dissi, "m' ha fatto il parlar dolce
e pio."* The present, *soave e leve,* does not retrospectively rein-
terpret the past, *Quant' io soffersi mai,* but opposes and sup-
plants it.

Undermining even the horizontal succession of meanings
and attracting critical attention more specifically to the interpretive or perceptual habits of the dreamer himself, there are a
whole range of such non sequiturs which serve throughout the
poem to intensify the kinds of interpretive conflict which the
larger movements somewhat crudely and ostentatiously appease.
Though each of the six triumphs—in order the *"Triumphus
cupidinis,"* the *"Triumphus pudicitie,"* the *"Triumphus mortis,"*
the *"Triumphus fame,"* the *"Triumphus temporis,"* and the
"Triumphus eternitatis"—appears to the dreamer to present an
alternative to the view or vision that precedes it (even the initial
"Triumphus cupidinis," it should be noted), it is especially
these oppositions that prove spurious as soon as they are exam-
ined closely. The splendid procession at the opening of the
"Triumphus cupidinis," for example, manages at once to cast
a great light (*una gran luce* [I. 11]) which dazzles, and a
gloomy pall (*l'aer fosco* [I. 46]) which obstructs, the dreamer's

vision. (One quickly understands why illustrators, in particular, ignored Petrarch's text when trying to visualize this apparition.) It has caused the dreamer to rejoice, yet it is filled with a dreariness which pointedly recalls his mood just prior to falling asleep:

> *Ivi fra l'erbe, già del pianger fioco,*
> *vinto dal sonno, vidi una gran luce*
> *e dentro assai dolor con breve gioco.*

> There, on the grass, already weak from weeping,
> overcome by sleep, I saw a great light and
> within much grief and little joy. (TC I, 10–12)

Once it is established that he will try to apprehend the nature of Love through learning about Love's captives, further problems arise. The figures themselves have, if anything, progressively less in common. At times they are grouped, like the lovers from Ovid's *Heroides,* according to a common literary source. Once the dreamer finds Love represented by two sets of figures who, except for their contiguity and equality in number, are diametrically opposed:

> *Vedi tre belle donne innamorate:*
> *Procri, Artemisia con Deidamia,*
> *ed altrettante ardite e scelerate:*
> *Semiramis, Bibli e Mirra ria.*

> I saw three beautiful, enamored ladies: Procris,
> Artemisia, and with them Deidamia, and just as many
> who were bold and wicked: Semiramis, Byblis, and
> evil Myrrha. (TC III, 73–76)

Conversely, the same figure may exemplify, in antithetical ways, two different concepts. Caesar, who goes in chains as a captive in Love's triumph, occupies the position of highest honor, next to the triumphatrix herself, in the *"Triumphus fame."* This semiotic instability is certainly compounded by, and perhaps partially attributable to, the intellectual and emotional limitations of the perceiver. What he has seen and felt attracted to can be completely incommensurable with what he has been capable of assimilating and narrating:

> *Era si pieno il cor di meraviglie*
> *ch'i stava come l'uom che non po dire,*
> *e tace, e guarda pur ch'altri 'l consiglie.*

My heart was so full of marvels that I was
like a man who cannot speak and falls silent
and watches for another to counsel him. (TC III, 1–3)

Once the dreamer feels he *does* understand the paradoxes
and contradictions of love, his comprehension proves to be the
most unreliable indicator of all. Captivated by an apparition of
his own beloved, he becomes quite literally a captive, one of the
prisoners in Love's train. Temporarily his new "knowledge," as
he calls it, liberates him from the past definite of time-bound
observations and allows him a thirty-five line interlude in an
ahistorical present:

> *Or so come da sé 'l cor si disgiunge*
> *e come sa far pace, guerra e tregua,*
> *e coprir suo dolor, quand' altri il punge;*
>
> · · · · · · · · · · · · · ·
>
> *so come sta tra' fiori ascoso l'angue,*
> *come sempre tra due si vegghia e dorme,*
> *come senza languir si more e langue.*

Now I know how the heart is separated from itself
and how it knows to make peace, war, and truce,
and to hide its grief, when another pierces it. . . .
I know how the serpent hides itself among the
flowers, how one always sleeps and wakes between
two contraries, how without suffering illness,
one may die and suffer. (TC III, 151–53, 157–59)

Not surprisingly, though, he soon finds himself trapped, not in
the past (or not only in the past), but in a particularly confin-
ing *tenebrosa e stretta gabbia* (TC IV, 157), a gloomy and
cramped cage, where Love's other followers no longer appear a
means to knowledge, but become instead mere empty images.

It is important at this point to consider the mechanism of
this entrapment as well as its consequences. The remaining five
trionfi are all called into being in one way or another by the
threat it poses. It happens for the first time at the moment when

the dreamer is wholly "captivated," when, in other words, he no longer has one eye on the *chiuso loco* and one on the dream landscape, but has had his focus shifted entirely into the dream. What was at first pertinent to him because of its difference from and apparent opposition to his waking state, finally usurps his entire field of vision. His heart has become, as he says he knows, separated from itself—*Or so come da sé 'l cor si disgiunge*—for his "understanding" is more accurately a forgetting of the relational aspect of the antithesis out of which a new sense of self and self-knowledge has been constituted.

It is the illusion of autonomy, of a self which provides the common ground for contraries and conflicts, to which the poem here addresses itself. For Petrarch the associations with this problem are Dantesque. The fatally compelling image of the dreamer's beloved appears just after Dante's Paolo and Francesca have been mentioned, and the dreamer's capitulation is similar to theirs. Dante's lovers, we recall, allowed the fiction of Lancelot and Guinivere to pre-empt the present moment of their reading of that fiction. By "forgetting" their own role in constituting the text in terms of which they chose to govern themselves, they, in a sense, made fictions of themselves. The structure of the *Commedia,* of course, comments ironically on this mode of self-definition. The couple's historically defined identities reassert themselves, appropriately, in the person of Francesca's husband who is also Paolo's brother. He cuts short their idyll, he and the Infernal context in which we hear this story casting the baselessness of the lovers' readings of themselves and of each other into relief.

The crucial difference between Paolo and Francesca and Petrarch's dreamer is that the latter's act of misreading seems to have been unavoidable. He has not "chosen." As in the story of Paolo and Francesca, self-entrapment is not the solution to the indeterminacy of experience, but Petrarch does not oppose, as Dante seems to, the possibility of a historically grounded self-reading to the purely fictive readings within which people imprison themselves. The dreamer's "punishment" is, in fact, emblematic of his situation before *and* after his captivation:

> *In così tenebrosa e stretta gabbia*
> *rinchiusi fummo, ove le penne usate*

mutai per tempo e la mia prima labbia;
  e 'ntanto, pur sognando libertate,
l'alma, che 'l gran desio fea pronta e leve,
consolai col veder le cose andate.
  Rimirando er'io fatto al sol di neve
tanti spirti e sì chiari in carcer tetro,
quasi lunga pittura in tempo breve,
  che 'l piè va innanzi e l'occhio torna a dietro.

In such a gloomy and cramped cage I was enclosed
where in the course of time I changed my accustomed
feathers and my first face, while, only dreaming
of liberty, I consoled my spirit, which my great
desire made impressionable and eager, with the
sight of by-gone things. I became like snow in the
sun, gazing at so many illustrious souls in the
gloomy prison, like a long picture seen in a short
time, such that the foot goes forward and the eye
turns back. (TC IV, 157–67)

Ever since Orpheus, the eye turning to look behind as the
dreamer's does has been emblematic of a kind of nostalgic reification which falsifies the power of metaphor to shape and to
motivate action. But here the dreamer is faced with a situation
in which *any* interpretive position yields a reification. Though
he does not deny time or history, whose passage manifests itself
in the signs of aging he notes, this "historical" self is itself an
ambiguous entity. *L'usate penne* and *la prima mia labbia* do not,
at any rate, distinguish between the covering of his head and
his writing implements, between facial features and the organ
which forms speech out of sound. As has been indicated, analogously, by his disinclination or inability to locate his story defi-
nitely in either the past tense of "event" or the present tense
of narration (the poem slips back and forth between the two
almost from the very beginning), the narrator or dreamer himself, at any and all points in the text, is hardly less "fictive"
than any part of his dream. Perhaps during such historical
times, in a century described as *voto d'ogni valor, pien d'ogni
orgoglio* (devoid of any value, full of every pretension [TC I,
18]), an "historically grounded self-reading" is necessarily indistinguishable from self-delusion; the "ground" in terms of

which this "self" is constituted is, in any case, the first cause of, rather than the solution to, the problem of self-positioning. Compounding the problem such a self becomes all the more vulnerable to the kind of stabilized and stabilizing illusion represented by the dreamer's pseudo-revelation. The dreamer's *libertate,* not excepting the liberation from his own *secol noioso* apparently effected by the initial stages of Love's triumph, has been a dream all along.

The absence of historical grounding is, in other words, a hermeneutic problem in the *Trionfi,* and not the *prima radice* of sin which the denial of historicity becomes in the *Commedia.* This problem is taken up again in all the succeeding *trionfi,* but the fifth *trionfo,* the *"Triumphus temporis,"* is perhaps the most immediately relevant. There the dreamer discovers that the kinds of order—political, intellectual, or artistic—that are made of experience are only as real as the infrastructure on which they depend, and that neither human authors nor that which they presume to authorize remain constant. The sun, the titular figure of the *trionfo,* saves his special ire for those who think to escape the common lot through their relatively durable political or poetic codifications of significance:

> *Vidi una gente andarsen queta queta*
> *senza temer di Tempo o di sua rabbia,*
> *che gli avea in guardia istorico o poeta.*
> *Di lor par che più d'altri invidia s'abbia,*
> *che per se stessi son levati a volo*
> *uscendo for della comune gabbia.*

> I saw a people going very quietly without
> fear of Time or of his wrath, because poets
> and historians were standing guard. Of these
> it appeared that the sun was most envious,
> since, escaping from the common cage, they had
> risen in flight through their own efforts. (TT, 88–93)

Once again, the escape is illusory. The more absolute or immutable or beautiful the construct seems, the more it falsifies and deceives. The dreamer hears a voice saying:

> *Passan vostre grandezze e vostre pompe,*
> *passan le signorie, passano i regni:*

ogni cosa mortal Tempo interrompe,
  e ritolta a' men buon, non dà a' più degni;
e non pur quel di fuori il Tempo solve,
ma le vostre eloquenzie e' vostri ingegni.

. . . .

  Or perché umana gloria à tante corna,
non è mirabil cosa, s'a fiaccarle
alquanto oltra l'usanza si soggiorna.

Your grandeur and displays pass away, your ruler-
ships pass and your kingdoms: Time interrupts
every mortal thing, and what it has retaken from
the less good, it does not give to the more worthy;
and Time does not dissolve only external things, but
your eloquence and your genius . . . only because
human glory has so many branches is it not surprising if to exhaust them all sometimes takes
longer than usual. (TT, 112–17, 121–23)

As in the *"Triumphus cupidinis,"* the satisfaction of definition,
the illusion of understanding, offer a baseless seduction. The
better, the more complex and comprehensive the metaphor, the
greater the lie. It is not just that these intellectual and spiritual ac-
complishments are perishable; they are useless, or worse yet, self-
defeating, as ways of apprehending and adapting to a world in
which the central fact is the absence of any ontological structure
of the sort implied by the "understandings" they present. The
voice heard by the dreamer is itself subject to a significant error.
The "interruption" or breaking off of mortal things attributed
to Time, itself an intellectual/linguistic construct, harks back
to the rupture or discontinuity which takes place between the
uncertainty of relational perception and the achievement of a
unifying interpretive position. Time may be a way of measuring
the extent of this rupture in historical terms, but its apparent
power, too, is a function of convention—*l'usanza.* Time does
not prove the lie of metaphor; it is a metaphor whose own discontinuity proves the lie of Time's would-be distinction between
presence and its passing (Passan *vostre grandezze e vostre
pompe,* / passan *le signorie,* passano *i regni*), and demonstrates
the equivalence (captured in the ambiguity of the Italian *il
Tempo solve*) of resolution and dissolution.

It is worth considering, at this point, the criticisms made of the poem by those critics who have maintained that Petrarch (in the fourteenth century) would have written this way only if he lacked the talent to do otherwise. What modern Petrarch scholars look for and fail to find in the *Trionfi* is an overarching design which would serve as a corrective for the narrator's limited and confusing phenomenological perspective, which would serve at least to distinguish Petrarch from the dreamer and the dreamer from the dream. Thomas Bergin, an astute reader of Petrarch, explains: "The basic flaw derives from a constitutional incapacity of Petrarch to handle the grand design. . . . Even on such a simple level as the narrative plane, his work lacks consistency; the central figure is partly narrator, partly actor, partly a man with a vision, partly commentator."[8] This is indeed the ambiguous position of the dreamer, and Bergin does a good job characterizing it. What he does not see is that this position is consistent with the other poetic strategies of the *Trionfi* and with its conceptual problematic. To distinguish a reliable narrator and a clear-cut narrative object would be to counteract all that the poem tries to accomplish. Were Petrarch to do so, he could indeed be accused of incompetence. Just as useful (and just as perfectly mistaken) is Umberto Bosco's criticism of Petrarch's descriptive power in the characterization of personnel and physical surroundings in the *Trionfi*. A battle scene between Amor and Laura, the titular figure in the *"Triumphus pudicitie,"* is but murkily rendered. We are given no description of the terrain, and Laura herself is described by a series of negative comparisons:

> *Non fan sì grande e sì terribil sono*
>
> *Non corse mai sì levemente al varco*
>
> *che giàmmai schermidor non fu sì accorto*
> *a schifar colpo, nè nocchier sì presto*
> *a volger nave dagli scogli in porto*
>
> *Non ebbe mai di vero valor dramma*
> *Camilla . . .*
>
> *non fu sì ardente Cesare in Farsaglia . . .*

Non fu 'l cader di subito sì strano
dopo tante vittorie ad Anniballe,

non freme così 'l mar quando s'adira,
non Inarime allor che Tifeo piange,
Né Mongibel s'Encelado sospira.

Never make so great and terrible a sound

Never ran so swiftly to the pass

Never was there a fencer so adept at dodging blows
nor pilot so ready to turn the ship from the reefs
in port.

Camilla's valor was no more than a dram

Caesar was not as ardent in Pharsalia

The sudden fall of Hannibal was not so strange

The sea does not rage thus when it is angry, nor Ischia
when Typhoeus weeps, nor Etna when Enceladus sighs.
(TP, 25, 37, 49–51, 70–71, 73, 97–98, 112–14)

By the end of the battle, Laura has been compared in this way
to a lion, a thunderbolt, a flame, a whirlwind, a deer fleeing a
leopard, a fencer dodging blows, a pilot who skillfully avoids
reefs, Camilla the amazon, Caesar, Scipio, David, and Judith.
Laura's characteristic gestures of aggressively avoiding, dodging, or consuming material objects and obstacles is missed by
Bosco, all of whose sensibilities are outraged: "I leave aside the
comparisons with which Love, her adversary, is blessed. All this
to say simply that Love bends his bow against Laura."[9] Bosco
ends by dismissing this excessive use of negatives as a flounder-
ing of the poet's imagination. That he can formulate no clear
picture of the scene and its action from this kind of description,
however, is one measure of its success as a stylistic *tour de force*
in the poem's own terms. The negative comparisons, especially,
represent an elegant refinement of the poem's general princi-

ple. No less than would positive comparisons, they evoke images
and associations, but the reader is simultaneously told he must
put them aside. The mind carries away impressions and atti-
tudes, but is not allowed to stop and dwell upon any of them.
The incompatibility of the similes with each other, except as
they doubly avoid the object, works toward the same end. It
protects Chastity's triumph against the kind of imaginative
assent that would be invited by more stable metaphors. What
both Bergin and Bosco at once see and do not see in the poem
is its concerted experimentation in *negative stylistics,* a subversion of the delicate yet tyrannical operations of a more usual,
but here inadequate, aesthetic sensibility.

Chastity herself, in fact, comes to represent resistance to
the coercion of style offered by more positive formulations, as
well as to the seduction of self-evident "truths" which an ele-
gantly polished, authoritative text might have to offer. Her de-
feat of Amor in the second *trionfo* is followed in the so-called
"Triumphus mortis" by a startling scene in which she takes
issue with the eloquent threats of the imposing black-robed
figure of Death, and it is Death who backs down. The poem
makes its point dramatically rather than didactically (to be
didactic would be to fall into one of the very modes it subverts)
by portraying their exchange in direct discourse. Death announces herself:

> *O tu, donna, che vai*
> *di gioventute e di bellezze altera,*
> *e di tua vita il termine non sai,*
>   *io son colei che sì importuna e fera*
> *chiamata son da voi, e sorda e cieca*
> *gente, a cui si fa notte innanzi sera;*
>
> . . . .
>
>   *Or a voi, quando il viver più diletta,*
> *drizzo 'l mio corso innanzi che Fortuna*
> *nel vostro dolce qualche amaro metta.*

Oh you, lady, who go proud of your youth and
beauty, and do not know when your life will end,
I am she who is called relentless and fierce by
you and by people blind and deaf, for whom night
comes before evening. . . . Now to you, when life

is most delightful, I direct my course before
Fortune adds any bitterness to your pleasure.
(TM I, 34–39, 46–48)

But Laura, the embodiment of rhetorical as well as physical
chastity, refuses to accept this formulation, especially as it im-
periously defines herself and her companions:

> In costor non ài tu ragione alcuna
> ed in me poca: solo in questa spoglia.
>
> . . . .
>
> Altri so che n'avrà più di me doglia,
> la cui salute dal mio viver pende;
> a me fia grazia che di qui me scioglia.

Over these with me you have no right and you
have very little over me; only over my bodily
garment. I know another who will grieve more
than I, whose well-being depends upon my life;
to me it were a blessing to be released from
here. (TM I, 49–50, 52–54)

Death, whose discourse was intended to subordinate the partial
view of her victims to her own more comprehensive view, has
the rug pulled out from under her by Laura's untroubled will-
ingness to shed such earthly "garments" altogether. As Laura
has further pointed out, Death can signify only to the living,
and it is the living who variously decide its significance. Death
stands corrected:

> Qual è chi 'n cosa nova gli occhi intende
> e vede ond' al principio non s'accorse,
> di ch'or si meraviglia e si riprende,
> tal si fe' quella fera . . .

As one who bends her eyes on something new
and sees what at first she had not noticed, at
which she marvels and corrects herself, such was
that fierce creature. (TM I, 55–58)

Laura's compassionate aside concerning the benighted poet who
will take Death at her word is perhaps Petrarch's ironic comment upon the writer's particular vulnerability to the power of

authoritative discourse. It is notable that Death is by far the more overtly "poetic" figure of the two, and that she behaves as if she could not properly *see* the less rhetorically pretentious Laura.

This poetry, though, is as aggressively and promiscuously chaste as Chastity/Laura herself. It is utterly innocent, for example, of structurally significant geographical or cosmological landmarks. The effortless translocations of the spectacle from a closed valley to Amor's palace/prison on Cyprus and to Chastity's temple in Rome via Scipio's solitary retreat at Literno are the opposite of the arduous step-by-step Dantesque account of descent and ascent. Petrarch's foreign scenes have a studio air about them. They are the same set with different names. Or as Bosco puts it, "if sometimes he describes, and it happens very rarely, it is always the landscape of Vaucluse"[10] (the site of Petrarch's most permanent home, and the setting of many of his poems). The numerous figures whom the dreamer encounters all share the same ground, or better, they share a kind of groundlessness. They occupy no particular place in the physical or moral universe. Similarly, the poem's *donnée,* that the spectator remains stationary relative to the transitory spectacle, suggests that Petrarch does not aspire to transcend the individual, subjective perspective. This conspicuous reversal of the Dantesque situation signals Petrarch's profound estrangement from the poetics of transcendence.

Very pointedly in the *"Triumphus eternitatis,"* where one might expect some panoramic cosmological ratification of the pilgrim's progress, the "vision" becomes instead completely interior:

> *Questo pensava, e mentre più s'interna*
> *la mente mia, veder mi parve un mondo*
> *novo, in etate immobile ed eterna.*

> This I was thinking, and while my mind goes
> into itself more deeply, I seem to see a new
> world, in an immobile and eternal state. (TE, 19–21)

The version of eternity which follows has more to do with the changes that the absence of "time" would make in the mental processes of perception and intellection than it does with what the mind might then perceive and understand. The poet locates his paradise grammatically and syntactically rather than cosmologically:

> Quel che l'anima nostra preme e 'ngombra:
> "dianzi, adesso, ier, diman, mattino e sera"
> tutti in un punto passeran com' ombra;
>   non avrà loco "fu" "sarà" né "era,"
> ma "è" solo, "in presente," ed "ora" ed "oggi"
> e sola "eternità" raccolta e 'ntera.

That which oppresses and encumbers us: "previously, now, yesterday, tomorrow, morning, evening," all these will pass like a shadow into one point; "was," "will be" and "used to be" will have no place, but only "is," "in the present" and "now" and "today" and only "eternity" gathered together and entire. (TE, 64–67)

In discussing the "Triumphus temporis" I noted that the voice heard by the dreamer was mistaken in attributing the insubstantialization of mortal things to time. The solution offered by Time to the problem of metaphor—everything passes away—denied the terms of the problem. The error recurs here, in the final trionfo, but in a significantly different form. Time, which I described earlier as "an intellectual/linguistic construct," is explicitly characterized now as an assemblage of grammatical and syntactic elements—adverbs, verb tenses, temporal nouns—which distinguish states of mind and carry the weight of senses of time. In other words, the rupture between the unstable perception of a persona and a unitary position, which was first analyzed apropos of the "Triumphus cupidinis" in rhetorical terms, is finally recast here as a grammatical problem. The "oppression" and "encumbrance" of uncertain relational moments is that of verb tenses, adverbs, and temporal nouns; and the "paradise" of a unified position which is aspired to is a language of presence, a language, that is, of the present tense ("is," "now," etc.). But, though the error need no longer be understood as one of rhetorical construction, the verbal sleight of hand that would grammatically heal the rupture is no less problematic. To arrive at—that is, to describe—this "place" or "position" is not to represent it, to present objects or a landscape, but to present a linguistic possibility, and yet the terms of this verbal presentation of a utopian language are the very terms which such a language would deny. The future tense "will have no place," the past tense "will [be] . . . *gathered*," and the sense of "gathered together entire" are non-sense without a sense of syntactic fragmentation and dispersal. The language which has "no place" for the temporality of grammar and syntax is, in fact, a "no place" (*u-topos*) in terms of that grammar and syntax.

It is specifically the ground for figural interpretation that Petrarch definitively dissolves by means of this final restatement of the problem, and he pointedly refers here to those, not unlike his persona in *Canzone* 23, who persist in trying to play the figural "game":

> *quasi spianati dietro e 'nnanzi i poggi*
> *ch'occupavan la vista, non fia in cui*
> *vostro sperare e rimembrar s'appoggi;*
> *la qual varietà fa spesso altrui*
> *vaneggiar sì che 'l viver pare un gioco,*
> *pensando pur: "che sarò io? che fui?"*

The hills having been flattened before and
behind which used to occupy the view, there
will not be that on which your hope and remem-
brance might lean; whose variation often makes
people rave so that to live appears a game, so
that they think only: "What shall I be? What
have I been?" (TE, 70–75)

The game referred to here is the play of difference (*varietà*) between two temporal positions which have just been shown to be equally insubstantial. The future is as much an optical illusion as the past. The subject and its present represent a compound version of this error. In order to define itself, to "mean" something, the subject at once constitutes and is constituted by a reification of the arbitrary syntactical relationship between these two positions.

Nonetheless, Petrarch, no more than Dante, attributes this "false" figural reification to the tradition of Christian figural interpretation. Petrarch's poetics discourages figural modes of thought and interpretation, not, I would infer, to foster secular nihilism, but to undercut the secular "reality" that Petrarch claims to find in de facto dominance in the world around him. The dream vision, we recall, is not finally separable from the unprepossessing historical situation out of which it arises; the uncertain perspective offered by this situation must itself be understood to be as partial and contingent as the perspective that might be achieved at any other moment. I would further support my inference by making some concluding observations about the feature of the poem which has proved the greatest stumbling block of all to modern readers.

More than half the poem is taken up with what are often remembered as heavy, monotonous catalogues. These catalogues occur in only three of the six *trionfi*—the *"Triumphus cupidinis,"* the *"Triumphus pudicitie,"* and the *"Triumphus fame"*—but they are often thought of as making up the entire work, and they apparently account for much of the literary historical confusion surrounding it. Readers like C. S. Lewis, who determines that "the whole plan of Petrarch's *Trionfi* seems to be devised for the purpose of admitting as many catalogues as possible," assume that Petrarch is ineptly using a rhetorical device commonly found in medieval literature.[11] Lewis suggests that medieval authors (among whom he includes Petrarch) presented encyclopedic information which most of their audience must already have known, and that they did so because author and audience alike found it aesthetically satisfying to dwell on the great imagined structure of their universe. "Every particular fact and story became more interesting and more pleasurable if, by being properly fitted in, it carried one's mind back to the Model as a whole."[12] Thus, although the catalogue was often identified in rhetorical terms as a digression or amplification, it might be regarded functionally as a highly economical means of filling in the total picture. The *Commedia,* the most sophisticated of medieval catalogues, is a supreme example of this economy. It is encyclopedic, not by virtue of naming all the constituents of each class, of being quantitatively comprehensive, but by outlining the articulations of a single, internally consistent system which makes intelligible each of its constituent parts.[13] On each Purgatorial terrace, for instance, one example of a virtue from the life of the Virgin, one from pagan history, and one from Christian history are sufficient to describe the nature of that virtue in terms of all of human history. Typically, the hierarchical arrangement of sins and virtues tells us enough about them that the poet is free to offer idiosyncratic *exempla* which demand more complicated responses than would the obvious or expected. Considering the scope of the poem, the number of what E. R. Curtius has called its "personnel" is surprisingly low.[14] A significant grouping of a few figures in fact tells us far more than a long list could.

The governing trope which Lewis identifies as characteristic of medieval discourse and which Dante uses so brilliantly is, of course, synecdoche, the substitution of the part for the whole, the species for the genus, or the genus for the species. This use of synecdoche depends upon and implies a whole system of hierarchically ordered (though not necessarily reified) relationships. It is a trope of *totalization.* Its prominence in medieval literature suggests, as Lewis says, a conception of the universe as a coherent totality. Conversely, our immunity to the potency of medieval catalogues may reflect both the changes that have occurred in our modes of conceptualization and the loss of the sense of intimacy with the "universe" that these changes have entailed.[15] Nevertheless, as Bergin's complaints about the catalogues in the *Trionfi* make clear, any age would be hard put to do without synecdoches of a less global sort. For Bergin, Petrarch "lacked the discretion (God's gift to Dante) to keep the informational drive under control."[16] In the *"Triumphus fame,"* "the enumeration seems endless, and the efforts of the poet to find phrases of individual definition or distinction are painful to observe."[17]

Bergin is quite right to sense that there is something very different about Petrarch's catalogues. Petrarch has gone out of his way, especially in his use of the catalogue, not to imply synecdochally the existence of a hierarchical system, a controlling idea, or a coherent universe. That his catalogues are exhaustive and exhausting, that his narrator must try to name *all* the figures in a given triumph, indicates the absence of any synecdochal understanding that would make this arduous, empirical approach to the whole unnecessary. And despite the length of the catalogues, Petrarch conscientiously avoids giving the impression that they ever succeed in being all-inclusive. In a moment of funny but poignant self-parody at the beginning of the second *capitolo* of the *"Triumphus fame,"* the poet compares his "vision" of eminent Romans to the "historical" texts on the basis of which their actions and reputations have traditionally been inferred, commenting that between those texts and his narrative there are large discrepancies:

> *giungea la vista con l'antiche carte*
> *ove son gli alti nomi e' sommi pregi,*
> *e sentiv'al mio dir mancar gran parte.*

> I compared what I saw with ancient documents
> where the great names and highest reputations
> are, and perceived that much was missing from
> my account. (TF II, 4–6)

This confrontation opens upon an infinite regression of discrepancies. The differences between Petrarch's textual fiction and those texts which are also (or have become) historical ones do not, on the one hand, even begin to approximate the difference or disjunction between those texts and the "realities" they preserve, nor can those "realities" themselves be said to escape the problems of textuality, understood in Petrarchan terms. The *alti nomi* or great *names* and the *sommi pregi* or highest *reputations* which "are" in the *antiche carte* exist at once nowhere else and not there either. On the other hand, we later learn in the *"Triumphus temporis"* that the "authorities" are incomplete in another way, due to losses incurred over the years. And, in any case, the dreamer is too quickly distracted by the appearance of a group of non-Roman notables, *pellegrini egregi,* for the *antiche carte* to be of much help in supplementing the Roman catalogue whose acknowledged incompleteness initiated this meditation. The dreamer has difficulty not only in naming the members of one species, but also in isolating one species from another. The pain and perplexity experienced by Bergin are his as well.

Nevertheless, the roll call of the illustrious is complete enough that certain figures are conspicuous by their absence, and we discover that the *lacunae* strikingly confirm what the disproportionate length and apparent raggedness of the catalogues imply. Bergin's scholarly wondering about Petrarch's

omissions probably approximates the reaction the poem intends
to provoke: "Whole catalogues of medieval worthies are ex-
cluded. There are no great kings: one might have expected St.
Louis at least, or, given our poet's devotion to the house of
Sicily, Charles of Anjou; and if philosophers, why not Christian
Saints?"[18] Here in ghostly form is the economy, the synecdochal
use of names and images, which Bergin misses and which Lewis
even more amazingly finds in the catalogues as given. The absence of the architects and defenders of the Christocentric
model signals the absence, already sensed in the calculated
shapelessness of the poem, of the model itself. The only trace
of the Christ event, the only occurrence of the name Christ, is
the mention of His empty tomb which the contemporary Christian world has abandoned to the Saracens:

> *gite superbi, o miseri Cristiani,*
> *consumando l'un l'altro, e non vi caglia*
> *che 'l sepolcro di Cristo è in man de' cani!*

> Continue in your pride, O wretched Christians,
> consuming one another, and let it not matter to
> you that the sepulchre of Christ is in the hands
> of dogs. (TF II, 142–44)

Christ is as doubly absent as the human subject which, for Augustine or Dante, could be defined in terms of Him; the absence of any other New Testament figures—there are only Old
Testament characters, mentioned in the *"Triumphus cupidinis"*
and the *"Triumphus fame"*—effectively brackets that chapter
of human history which had traditionally been appealed to in
making sense of the rest.[19]

The critical interest in the *Trionfi* as a "medievalizing"
and ultimately confessional poem is, therefore, misplaced. The
poem's few apparently Christian elements occur in the form of
empty pieties which serve merely to obscure (for the poem's
personae) the consequences of defining the self and its world
in exclusively secular terms. On the other hand, it is not necessarily a "modernist" secular poem either; it would not substitute
an understanding of linguistic and rhetorical operations for
religious understanding. The misimpression that my reading
could possibly convey is that Petrarch, in subverting figural in-

terpretation, is subverting only or chiefly Christian figural interpretation. The "new field of vision," or cultural alternative
suggested by the rediscovery and revaluation of classical texts
(and evoked most powerfully in the opening *trionfo*), serves, it
might seem, simply to burst the bounds of a unified theological-
historiographical system of belief. It is precisely this abuse of
the "new learning," though, toward which the poetics of the
Trionfi is consistently directed. A new poetics of history and
therefore of narrative needs to be worked out, not in order to
reduce Christian history to a mere chapter in a larger volume of
historiographical schemata (the option obliquely presented in
the episode of Massinissa and Sophonisba and later indirectly
criticized in the dream-within-a-dream of Laura after her death),
but rather in order to deconstruct *merely* historical understandings of past and present. The point the *Trionfi* makes, in other
words, is that *any* historical understanding is inevitably figural,
that a new historical understanding replaces one set of metaphorical possibilities with another. To the extent that this irre-
ducible metaphoricity is not understood, historical "knowledge"
becomes at best a deception and at worst the agency of moral,
spiritual, and perhaps political paralysis. To claim or to appear
to claim completeness for one's reading of the past, and, by
extension, for one's reading of oneself, is to enlist history in
precisely the causes to which it is least suited: those of endow-
ing the moment of discourse with a privileged status, and of
masking (or repressing) the ambiguity of its "meaning."

Afterword

In these discussions of Petrarch's Italian poetry, I have urged that a literary-historical understanding of its stylistic features and rhetorical structures could serve the interests of today's theoretical discussions of meaning, and yet I have uncovered a deconstruction of such historical understanding in the texts themselves. An investigation of the relationship of Petrarch's poetics to the poetics of the *Commedia* closes with a discussion of the structural relationship between the "historical self" and its narratives, which I have found it useful to conceptualize in terms of Narcissistic mirroring. The attempt to retrieve and locate the *Trionfi* as a constituent element of a literary history which should concern us for the persistent differences it poses from its own literary tradition and from our more immediate literary past, devolves into an analysis of how the question of temporal and conceptual position becomes cast as an insoluble grammatical problem in the *"Triumphus eternitatis."* My argument remains, though, that once Petrarch's poetry is shown to be involved in or to enact many of the same issues that theoretical discussions often treat ahistorically, the question of "history" becomes relevant to these discussions. The issues "mean" something in Petrarch's poetry because of the relational context in which they evolve and appear, and furthermore, their "meaning" is available only when arrived at through a relational reading which is historical (even when it involves only Petrarch and his immediate predecessor, Dante). In this relational reading one encounters a kind of irreversibility principle. For example, we have seen that it becomes impossible for Petrarch to write like Arnaut without writing differently from him because of the mutually constituting relationship of Petrarch to Dante that intervenes. "History," if so we wish to name a kind of difference, and repetition of the same, would appear to be mutually exclusive.

The fact that this study itself is implicated in the Narcissistic problematic of narrative-historical understanding that I have presented with respect to Petrarch's *Canzone* 23 should further explain and justify, rather than undercut, my attempt to define more precisely the historical questions which might be asked, and the historiographical tools which might be used in coming to terms with the strategies of positing and positioning "literary-historical" selves (as well as our own "critical-historical" ones). The theoretical questions which could be posed at this point are whether or not historical-relational understanding remains called for in further treatments of the problems raised by the Petrarchan text, and whether or not Petrarch's poetry may be taken to offer a significant historical difference in the uncovering and presentation of poetic and rhetorical problems. I would comment upon these questions as follows: if the narrative unfolding of a poetic relationship, which is finally understood to have its non-narrative aspect, has been necessary in order to arrive at a way of talking about the structure of a poetic "change" that implies the possibility of a "shift" in the way the signifying possibilities of language are used, it would seem to have served a cause that would only be betrayed if that narrative were not admitted to be itself instrumental, contingent, and figural. Conversely, though, without the narrative-historical understanding, the theoretical perspective risks a Narcissistic fixation on *its* own logic which might prevent it, in turn, from realizing the means by which it was developed, and its own further potential.

Notes

Chapter I

1. Theodor E. Mommsen, "Petrarch's Conception of the 'Dark Ages,' " *Speculum* 17 (April 1942):226–42.
2. John Freccero, "The Fig Tree and the Laurel: Petrarch's Poetics," *Diacritics* 5, 1 (1975):34–40.
3. Ibid., 38–39.
4. Thomas M. Greene's "Petrarch and the Humanist Hermeneutic," in *Italian Literature, Roots and Branches: Essays in Honor of Thomas Godard Bergin,* ed. Giose Rimanelli and John Achity (New Haven: Yale University Press, 1976) is the notable exception. Greene does find the poetry and the prose texts mutually illuminating, and my own argument is much indebted both to the thesis of his essay and to the sensitive readings with which he supports his argument.
5. Mario Emilio Cosenza, *Francesco Petrarca and the Revolution of Cola di Rienzo* (Chicago: The University of Chicago Press, 1913), pp. 318, 323–24.
6. These operations could, then, be compared to the operation of difference in the constitution of any meaning. This description is indebted to Jacques Derrida's argument concerning writing and difference in *De la grammatologie* (Paris: Les Editions de Minuit, 1967), esp. pp. 38–39.
7. For the opinion that Petrarch was not a systematic thinker, see Charles Trinkaus, *"In Our Image and Likeness"* (London: Constable and Co., 1970), vol. 1, pp. 4–5. Because of Petrarch's silence on the matters of natural philosophy and cosmology which play so prominent a role in the systems of earlier medieval and later Renaissance thinkers, Trinkaus concludes, "To Petrarch the irrelevance of both physics and metaphysics was almost absolute;

he couldn't have cared less." However, the fact that Petrarch found the physical and moral universe undecipherable could as well be taken as a sign of his philosophical rigor as of its opposite. Trinkaus also finds Petrarch's understanding of rhetoric "psychologically effective but epistemologically irrelevant" in his recent study, *The Poet as Philosopher: Petrarch and the Formation of Renaissance Consciousness* (New Haven: Yale University Press, 1979), p. 29. In this volume Trinkaus gives more credit to Petrarch as a historian of philosophy than as a thinker in his own right, repeatedly attributing to him intuitive, rather than systematically achieved, insights.

8. Jacob Burckhardt, *The Civilization of the Renaissance in Italy* (New York: The New American Library of World Literature, 1960), p. 121.

9. Roland Barthes, "To Write: Intransitive Verb?," in *The Structuralist Controversy: The Languages of Criticism and the Sciences of Man,* ed. Richard Macksey and Eugenio Donato (Baltimore: The Johns Hopkins Press, 1972), p. 150. This comment, made in response to a challenge by Paul de Man of Barthes' own conception of literary history, occurs in the "Discussion" following Barthes' paper.

10. Raffaele Amaturo, *Petrarca* (Roma-Bari: Editori Laterza, 1974), p. 86.

11. Mommsen, "Petrarch's Conception of the 'Dark Ages,' " p. 227.

12. In Book II of Petrarch's Latin epic, the *Africa,* Lucius Scipio breaks off his prophecy of Rome's future with the reigns of the Emperors Vespasian and Titus, saying, "I cannot bear to proceed; for strangers of Spanish and African extraction will steal the sceptre and the glory of the Empire founded by us with great effort. Who can endure the thought of the seizure of supreme control by these dregs of the people, these contemptible remnants, passed over by our sword?" (*ll.* 274–78), quoted from Mommsen, "Petrarch's Conception of the 'Dark Ages,' " pp. 234–35.

13. Mommsen, "Petrarch's Conception of the 'Dark Ages,' " p. 237. Petrarch's line is from the *Apologia contra cuiusdam anonymi Galli calumnias.*

14. Saint Augustine, *On Christian Doctrine,* trans. and with an introduction by D. W. Robertson, Jr., The Library of Liberal Arts, No. 80 (New York: The Liberal Arts Press, 1958), p. 84.

15. See ibid., pp. 84–86, where Augustine compares and contrasts Jewish literal-mindedness with Gentile idolatry.

16. Jacques Derrida, "La structure, le signe et le jeu," in *L'écriture et la différence* (Paris: Editions du Seuil, 1967), p. 410. The French text reads: *On a donc toujours pensé que le centre, qui par définition est unique, constituait, dans une structure, cela même qui, commandait la structure, échappe à la structuralité. C'est pourquoi, pour une pensée classique de la structure, le centre peut être dit, paradoxalement, dans la structure et hors de la structure. Il est*

au centre de la totalité et pourtant, puisque le centre ne lui appartient pas, la totalité a son centre ailleurs. The translation is taken from "Structure, Sign, and Play in the Discourse of the Human Sciences," in Macksey and Donato, *The Structuralist Controversy,* p. 248.

17. All quotations from Petrarch's correspondence are taken from *Le familiare,* ed. Vittorio Rossi, 4 vols. (Florence: Sansoni, 1933–42). Letters are identified by volume and number according to Petrarch's original division. The Latin text of the line quoted reads: *Quis enim dubitare potest quin illico surrectura sit, se ceperit se Roma cognoscere? Fam.* VI, 2. Translated by Mommsen, "Petrarch's Conception of the 'Dark Ages,'" p. 232.

18. Freccero, "The Fig Tree and the Laurel," p. 39.

19. Ibid., 39.

20. Ibid., 39 (footnote 3).

21. Umberto Eco, "The poetics of the open work," trans. Bruce Merry, *Twentieth Century Studies: The Limits of Comprehension* (Edinburgh, Scotland: Scottish Academic Press Limited, 1974), p. 11.

22. For example, one lesson taught by the elaborate language game of the *Canzoniere* becomes explicit in the great political *Canzone* CXXVIII, *"Italia mia."* Urging a kind of proto-nationalism in place of the dream of empire which had been Dante's political ideal, he exhorts: *Latin sangue gentile, / Sgombra da te queste dannose some; / non far idolo un nome / vano senza soggetto* (O gentle Latin blood, disencumber yourself of this harmful burden. Do not make an idol of a name which is empty and without subject). Petrarch does not absorb or accept, as Dante does, the gap between the ideal of the Holy Roman Empire and its unprepossessing reality. For him a shared name gives a strife-torn, pluralistic aggregate of peoples a false unity which deceives the Italian people to their detriment. Politics and poetics are inextricably mixed here.

23. *Fam.* VI, 2. . . . *[S]ic philosophica, sic poetica, sic historias legamus, ut semper ad aurem cordis Evangelium Cristi sonet: quo uno satis docti ac felices; sine quo quanto plura didicerimus, tanto indoctiores atque miseriores futuri sumus; ad quod velut ad summam veri arcem referenda sunt omnia; cui, tanquam uni literarum verarum immobili fundamento, tuto superedificat humanus labor.* . . . Translated by Mommsen, "Petrarch's Conception of the 'Dark Ages,'" pp. 231–32.

24. Greene, "Petrarch and the Humanist Hermeneutic," p. 201.

25. Both Rome and her Empire, according to Dante, were established in preparation for the establishment of the Papacy (*Inf.* II, 22–27). In other words, pagan and Christian Roman history made up a totality whose true meaning, whether before or after the conversion of Constantine, had always been the same. The consequences of the coming of Christ had simply made that meaning manifest.

26. *Fam.* VI, 2. *[Q]uas ita partiti videbamur, ut in novis tu, in antiquis ego viderer expertior.* Translated by Mommsen, "Petrarch's Conception of the 'Dark Ages,' " p. 232. For an extended discussion of another instance in the *Familiares* of Petrarch's problematic presentation of typological structures, see Robert M. Durling's "The Ascent of Mt. Ventoux and the Crisis of Allegory," *Italian quarterly* 18, 69 (Summer 1974):7–28.

27. Quotations from Petrarch's *Secretum* are taken from *Opere di Petrarca,* ed. Giovanni Ponte (Milan: U. Mursia and C., 1968). Passages are identified by book and page number. Translations, unless otherwise identified, are taken from *Petrarch's Secret,* trans. William H. Draper (London: Chatto and Windus, 1811). The Latin text of the phrase quoted reads: . . . *cui, non segnius quam Amphyon ille dirceus, in extremo occidentis summoque Atlantis vertice habitationem clarissimam atque pulcerrimam mirabili artificio ac poeticis, ut proprie dicam, manibus erexisti. Secretum,* Proem, p. 432.

28. Petrarch quotes the *Aeneid,* Book I, 327–28, exactly. See Vergil, *Eclogues, Georgics, Aeneid, 1–6,* trans. H. R. Fairclough, The Loeb Classical Library, vol. 1 (Cambridge, Mass.: Harvard University Press, 1974), p. 264 and *Secretum,* Proem, p. 432. The translation is mine.

29. *Secretum,* Book III, p. 540. . . . *Creatorem non qua decuit amasti, sed miratus artificem fuisti quasi nichil ex omnibus formosius creasset, cum tamen ultima pulcritudinum sit forma corporea.* Augustinus opens this round of the debate by making the charge in terms which pointedly recall Augustine's definition of literal understanding: *Ab amore celestium elongavit animum et a Creatore ad creaturam desiderium inclinavit. Que una quidem ad mortem pronior fuit via.* (She has detached your mind from the love of heavenly things and has inclined your heart to love the creature more than the Creator: and that one path alone leads, sooner than any other, to death.) His failure actually to invoke the doctrine a few lines later is thus made all the more surprising.

30. *Secretum,* Book III, p. 542.

> Ag. *Me ne ludis? An si idem animus in squalido et nodoso corpore habitaret, similiter placuisset?*
>
> Fr. *Non audeo quidem id dicere; neque enim animus cerni potest, nec imago corporis talem spopondisset; at si oculis appareret, amarem profecto pulcritudinem animi deforme licet habentis habitaculum.*
>
> Ag. *Verborum queris adminicula; si enim nonnisi quod oculis apparet amare potes, corpus igitur amasti.*

Translation mine.

31. *Secretum,* Book III, p. 550. . . . *[Q]uis digne satis execretur aut stupeat hanc alienate mentis insaniam, cum, non minus nominis*

quam ipsius corporis splendore captus, quicquid illi consonum fuit incredibili vanitate coluisti? Quam ob causam tanto opere sive cesaream sive poeticam lauream, quod illa hoc nomine vocaretur, adamasti; ex eoque tempore sine lauri mentione vix ullum tibi carmen effluxit, non aliter quam si vel Penei gurgitis accola vel Cirrei verticis sacerdos existeres. Denique quia cesaream sperere fas non erat, lauream poeticam, quam studiorum tuorum tibi meritum promittebat, nichilo modestius quam dominam ipsam adamaveras concupisti. Translation mine.

32. All quotations from Dante's *Commedia* are taken from *The Divine Comedy,* trans. with a commentary by Charles S. Singleton, Bollingen Series LXXX, 6 vols. (Princeton: Princeton University Press, 1970–75). Passages are identified by canticle, canto, and line. Translations are Singleton's.

33. *Secretum,* Book III, p. 552. *Cui consilio et magister amoris Naso consentit, regulam afferens generalem quod: "successore novo vincitur omnis amor." Et procul dubio sic est. Disgregatus et in multa distractus animus segnior vertitur ad singula. Sic Ganges, ut aiunt, a rege Persarum innumerabilibus alveis distinctus, atque ex uno metuendoque flumine in multos spernendos rivulos sectus est. Sic sparsa acies penetrabilis hosti redditur; sic diffusum lentescit incendium, denique omnis vis, ut unita crescit, sic dispersa minuitur.* Translation mine.

34. *Secretum,* Book III, pp. 552–54. *At contra quid hic michi videatur intellige. Valde siquidem metuendum est ne, dum ex una eaque (si dici fas est) nobiliori passione subtraheris, dilaberis in plurimas, et ex amante mulierosus vagus et instabilis fias; meo nempe iudicio si inevitabiliter pereundum sit, nobiliori morbo perisse solatium est. Quid igitur consulam, queres. Colligere animum et effugere, si possis, ac de carcere in carcerem commigrare non improbo. Spes enim forsitan in transitu libertatis fuerit, aut levioris imperii. Ereptum vero uni iugo collum per infinita sordidorum servitiorum genera circumferre non laudo.* Translation mine.

35. It is, I think, one of Petrarch's more accessible ironic gestures that the figure of Augustinus, the Church father, is made the spokesperson for the more radical propositions in the passages I have been discussing, while Franciscus, the ambitious, young love poet, is portrayed as the traditionalist, the conserver of the (now) empty form or structure of Augustinian interpretation. The question with which we opened this investigation—the question of what is new and what is not, of what about Petrarch's writing represents "change," and of how to describe that change—is, here as well as elsewhere in Petrarch's writing, to be found already inscribed within the text, in representations such as this one which confound the terms in which the question is posed. Here, for example, what is old chronologically—the desire for what both the historical Augustine and Petrarch's Augustinus call "freedom" —seems still to be the essence of a "new" poetic autonomy whose

newness may itself, however, be read as old-fashioned "idolatry," or as a disruption of the Augustinian doctrine of letter and spirit, or as a defense against the nature of language itself, comparable to, though different from, Augustinian theology, to name only three possibilities.

36. All citations from the *Canzoniere* follow Francesco Petrarca, *Canzoniere,* critical text and introduction by Gianfranco Contini and annotated by Daniele Ponchiroli (Torino: Einaudi, 1968). Passages are identified by their number in the series of 366 and by line. Translations are mine.

37. Ugo Foscolo, *Essays on Petrarch* (London: John Murray, 1823), p. 70.

Chapter II

1. All citations from Dante's *Commedia* are quoted from Dante Alighieri, *The Divine Comedy,* trans. with a commentary by Charles S. Singleton, Bollingen Series LXXX, 6 vols. (Princeton: Princeton University Press, 1970–75). Passages are identified by canticle, canto, and line. Translations are Singleton's unless otherwise noted.

2. Charles S. Singleton, *Commedia: Elements of Structure,* Dante Studies 1 (Cambridge, Mass.: Harvard University Press, 1954), pp. 89–90.

3. All citations from Scripture are quoted from the Vulgate Bible. The edition used here is the *Biblia Sacra,* Vulgate Editionis Sixti V Pontificis Maximi et Clementis VIII Auctoritate Edita (Rome: Editiones Paulinae, 1957). Passages are identified by book, chapter, and verse. The Latin text of the passage quoted above is: *Accipe librum et devora illum, et faciet amaricari ventrum tuum, sed in ore tuo erit dulce tanquam mel.* The translation is mine.

4. Ibid. The Latin text reads: *Fili hominis, venter tuus comedet, et viscera tua complebuntur volumine isto quod ego do tibi. Et comedi illus, et factum est in ore meo sicut mel dulce.* The translation is mine.

5. I am indebted to lectures by Professor John Freccero of Yale University for the recognition of this chain of allusions.

6. Giuseppe Mazzotta, "Poetics of History: Inferno XXVI," *Diacritics* 5, 2 (1975):41. See also chapter five, "Literary History," in Mazzotta's *Dante, Poet of the Desert* (Princeton: Princeton University Press, 1979). I regret that this dense, subtle, painstaking, and brilliant study of the *Commedia* appeared only as my own work was nearing completion, and that I have not, therefore, been able to draw upon its general argument and its particular readings to the extent I would have liked.

7. Giovanni Giudici, "Signor Petrarca, permette che la intervisti?,"

L'Espresso 18 (5 May 1974):63. . . . *un lessico tra i più mono-cordi d'ogni letterature . . . uno stile i cui movimenti richiedono a volte, per essere percepiti, una sensibilità sismografica.* Translation mine.

8. Ugo Foscolo comments upon Petrarch's habit of singing his verses and quotes Petrarch's Latin memoranda to that effect in his *Essays on Petrarch* (London: John Murray, 1823), pp. 57, 91. For evidence of Petrarch's revisions of the poems of the *Canzoniere,* see Ernest Hatch Wilkins, *The Making of the "Canzoniere" and Other Petrarchan Studies* (Rome: Edizioni di storia e letteratura, 1951), especially the title essay. For the argument that some of these revisions appear based upon formal considerations see Ruth Shepard Phelps' older study, *The Earlier and Later Forms of Petrarch's "Canzoniere"* (Chicago: The University of Chicago Press, 1925), pp. 185–88.

9. All citations from the *Canzoniere* follow Francesco Petrarca, *Canzoniere,* critical text and introduction by Gianfranco Contini and annotated by Daniele Ponchiroli (Torino: Einaudi, 1968). Translations are from *Petrarch's Lyric Poems,* trans. and ed. Robert M. Durling (Cambridge, Mass.: Harvard University Press, 1976) except where I indicate that they are my own. Passages are identified by their number in the series of 366 and by line.

10. Glauco Cambon, *Dante's Craft: Studies in Language and Style* (Minneapolis: The University of Minnesota Press, 1969), p. 197.

11. Harold Bloom, *A Map of Misreading* (New York: Oxford University Press, 1975), pp. 3 and 75, respectively.

12. In his recent study of Wallace Stevens, Bloom has specifically addressed himself to "disjunctions" or "poetic crossings" in the careers of individual poets. It is to be inferred from his discussion there that "a leaping of the gap between one kind of figurative thinking and another," when it occurs between two poets, need not indicate the impossibility of reading relationally any more than it does when it occurs between two poems by the same poet or within a single poem. See Harold Bloom, *Wallace Stevens: The Poems of Our Climate* (Ithaca, N.Y.: Cornell University Press, 1977), esp. p. 2.

13. Juliet Mitchell in her interpretation of Freud emphasizes this dimension of the Freudian father, and stresses the context in which the Oedipus complex occurs as largely constitutive of its local or immediate significance. She also comments on "the prevalent and fatal mistake of substituting the actual father for the father's function." See Juliet Mitchell, *Psychoanalysis and Feminism* (1974; rpt. New York: Vintage, 1975), esp. pp. 380, 392.

14. Cf. Bloom's objections to this kind of revision in *A Map of Misreading,* pp. 76–77.

15. Both projects, the quest for what is universal to Western poetics and the desire to discern significant shifts and changes, seem to me equally legitimate. The reader of literary history finally *chooses*

his or her object of study; neither the universal nor the differential view need imply that there is some truth intrinsic to literary texts which belies the other. Thus I do not in essence disagree with Bloom's recognition that "the affliction of belatedness . . . is a recurrent malaise of Western consciousness" (ibid., p. 77). I would simply wish to distinguish between different structures and valences of poetic influence. For an excellent discussion of the terms "change" and "crisis" as they apply to historical process, and as they are applied by and to critical theory, see the first chapter, "Criticism and Crisis," of Paul de Man's *Blindness and Insight: Essays in the Rhetoric of Contemporary Criticism* (New York: Oxford University Press, 1971), esp. pp. 6, 8, 16–19.

16. Hayden White, "The Problem of Change in Literary History," *New Literary History* 7 (1975):108.

17. Cf. John Freccero, "The Fig Tree and the Laurel: Petrarch's Poetics," *Diacritics* 5, 1 (1975):39.

18. Sara Sturm, "The Poet-Persona in the *Canzoniere,*" in *Francis Petrarch, Six Centuries Later: A Symposium,* North Carolina Studies in the Romance Languages and Literatures: Symposia, 3, ed. Aldo Scaglione (Chapel Hill and Chicago: Department of Romance Languages, University of North Carolina and The Newberry Library, 1975), p. 193.

19. Ibid., pp. 193–94.

20. For a differently argued but compatible discussion of the uncertain status of the moral language in Sonnet 1, see Giuseppe Mazzotta, "The *Canzoniere* and the Language of the Self," *Studies in Philology* 75, 3 (1978):271–72.

21. Dante writes, *io spero di dire di lei quello che mai non fue detto d'alcuna.* Quoted from Dante Alighieri, *La Vita Nuova,* con introduzione, commento e glossario di Giovanni Melodia (Milano: Dottor Francesco Vallardi, 1905), p. 266.

22. Cf. Jacques Derrida's exhaustive discussions of the problematic of speech and writing as he discovers it played out in Lévi-Strauss' chapter "Leçon d'écriture" in *Tristes Tropiques,* several texts of Rousseau, and Plato's *The Phaedrus,* to name only some of the instances he has chosen to explicate. See "La violence de la lettre: de Lévi-Strauss à Rousseau" and "Ce dangereux supplément . . . ," in *De la grammatologie* (Paris: Les Editions de Minuit, 1967), pp. 149–234; and especially "La pharmacie de Platon," in *La dissémination* (Paris: Editions du Seuil, 1972), pp. 69–197.

23. Mazzotta, "Poetics of History," pp. 39–40.

24. See Erich Auerbach, "Figura" (1939), in *Scenes from the Drama of European Literature,* trans. Ralph Manheim (New York: Meridian Books, 1959), pp. 11–76.

25. Leslie Fiedler, *No! in Thunder: Essays on Myth and Literature* (Boston: Beacon Press, 1960), p. 24. Fiedler is speaking mainly, however, of Dante's *sestina "Al poco giorno e al gran cerchio d'ombra."*

26. Adelia Noferi, *L'esperienza poetica del Petrarca* (Firenze: Felice le Monier, 1962), p. 4.

27. See also Roger Dragonetti, "The Double Play of Arnaut Daniel's *Sestina* and Dante's *Divina Commedia*," *Yale French Studies* 55/56 (1977):227–41 for a discussion of the poetics of the earliest extant *sestina*. Dragonetti suggests, among other things, that Arnaut Daniel's *sestina* "ends in the suppression of all hierarchy within the rhymes" (233) and, similarly, that "the rotation of the rhymes provokes a semantic circulation such that each rhyme word winds up becoming the mirroring of all the others" (237).

28. Noferi, *L'esperienza poetica del Petrarca*, pp. 13–14.

29. John Preston Brenkman, "Narcissus in the Text: Toward an Analysis of the Literary Subject in Ovid, Petrarch, and Yeats," Dissertation, The University of Iowa, 1974, p. 107.

30. Robert M. Durling, *The Figure of the Poet in Renaissance Epic* (Cambridge, Mass.: Harvard University Press, 1965), p. 84.

31. See also Roger Dragonetti's interesting hypothesis that a conception of literature implicit in Arnaut's *sestina* is reflected and reflected upon pervasively in the *Commedia:* e.g., "If Dante places the 'better craftsman of the mother tongue' at the very top of the steps of Purgatory—that is Arnaut Daniel who had practiced the poetics of heights so as better to imitate the distance of his narcissistic desire from the diversion of the high lady—it is that Dante recognized in this religion of *la fin'Amor* an art of divine resemblance in which St. Bernard, the Christian mystic, alone could challenge Arnaut at the summit of Paradise." Dragonetti, "The Double Play of Arnaut Daniel's *Sestina* and Dante's *Divina Commedia*," p. 245.

32. Quoted from *Anthology of the Provençal Troubadours*, ed. R. T. Hill and T. G. Bergin, revised and enlarged by Thomas Bergin, Susan Olson, William Paden, Jr., Nathaniel Smith (New Haven: Yale University Press, 1973), vol. 1, p. 104.

33. This point is implicit in my discussion of Cacciaguida and is also the sense of an important speech made by Adam in *Paradiso* XXVI. Adam says that language had changed long before Nimrod attempted to build the Tower of Babel. By this he indicates that there never was a timeless, privileged human language which incarnated Being more fully or more directly and transparently than another.

> *La lingua ch'io parlai fu tutta spenta*
> *innanzi che a l'ovra inconsummabile*
> *fosse la gente di Nembròt attenta:*
> *ché nullo effetto mai razionabile,*
> *per lo piacere uman che rinovella*
> *seguendo il cielo, sempre fu durabile.*

The tongue which I spoke was all extinct before
the people of Nimrod attempted their unaccomplish-

able work; for never was any product of reason
durable forever, because of human liking, which
alters, following the heavens. (*Par.* XXVI, 124–29)

The building of the Tower of Babel, a major attempt to bridge
the gap between the contingent and the absolute, is emblematic not
of a "fall" of language, but of a misunderstanding of the diacriti-
cal nature of signification, and hence of the proper relationship
between language and experience.

34. Bergin, *Anthology of the Provençal Troubadours,* p. 102. Transla-
tion adapted from *Lyrics of the Troubadours and Trouveres: An
Anthology and a History,* trans. and introductions by Frederick
Goldin (New York: Anchor/Doubleday, 1973), p. 219.

35. For a listing of Bloom's revisionary ratios, see *The Anxiety of Influence: A Theory of Poetry* (New York: Oxford University Press,
1973), pp. 14–16.

36. Wilkins, pp. 186, 188–89. I do not agree, however, with Wilkins'
claims in these pages that due to the piece-meal construction of
the *Canzoniere* "the exercise of artistic control over the final arrangement of the addenda as a whole was obviously impossible,"
and that with the additions of new poems the sense of the two-
part division of the sequence "remains . . . with diminished
strength."

37. Carlo Calcaterra, *Nella selva del Petrarca* (Bologna: Editore
Licinio Cappelli, 1942), esp. pp. 8–18, 44, 50–55, 210–26.

38. Umberto Bosco, *Petrarca* (Torino: Unione Tipografico-Editrice
Torinese, 1946), see esp. pp. 9–14, 166–70.

39. Aldo Scaglione, "La struttura del *Canzoniere* e il metodo di composizione del Petrarca," *Lettere Italiane* 27, 5 (1975):129–30.

40. Ibid., 139. English translation mine. Scaglione writes, . . . *non
sarebbe affatto illegittimo leggere il Petrarca come annunciatore di
posizioni "moderne," tenendo conto delle sue forme artistiche e del
loro rapporto con la sua psicologia dell'ambiguità metodica e la
sua visione di un mondo contraddittorio e dissociato.*

41. Scaglione, "La struttura del *Canzoniere*," p. 129. Scaglione cites
here Gianfranco Contini, *Saggio d'un commento alle correzioni del
Petrarca volgare* (Firenze: Sansoni, 1943), p. 7.

42. Thomas Roche, Jr., "The Calendrical Structure of Petrarch's *Canzoniere*," *Studies in Philology* 71, 2 (1974):152–72.

43. Ibid., 152.

44. Ibid., 155.

45. Ibid., 159.

46. For an important discussion of the different poetics of Dante's
three *cantiche,* see Francis X. Newman, "St. Augustine's Three
Visions and the Structure of the *Commedia*," *MLN* 82 (1967):
56–78.

47. For the following explanations and illustrations of the three-
sphere, I am indebted to Professor Mark Peterson of the Physics

Department at Amherst College. For the identification of the geometrical figure being described in *Paradiso* XXVIII as a sphere in four dimensions see Peterson's "Dante and the 3-sphere," *American Journal of Physics* 47, 12 (December 1979):1031–35.

Mathematically one can describe the 0-sphere, 1-sphere, 2-sphere, etc., as spaces in 1, 2, 3, etc., dimensions by equations:

(0) $x^2 = R^2$ (0-sphere)
(1) $x^2 + y^2 = R^2$ (1-sphere, or circle)
(2) $x^2 + y^2 + z^2 = R^2$ (2-sphere, or sphere in the ordinary sense)
(3) $x^2 + y^2 + z^2 + w^2 = R^2$ (3-sphere, a locus in four dimensions)

R is the "radius" of the sphere in each case. In particular, the 3-sphere which we are trying to describe can be pictured as "made up of" ordinary 2-spheres. To see this, fix w in equation (3) to have some temporarily constant value. The points x, y, z which satisfy (3) satisfy $x^2 + y^2 + z^2 = R^2 - w^2$. That is, they lie on a 2-sphere of radius $\sqrt{R^2 - w^2}$. Now by taking different values of w between R and $-R$ we map out the entire 3-sphere as a sequence of 2-spheres which increase until $w = 0$ and then decrease again to a point. (This is the crux of Dante's vision.) This construction is analogous to regarding the 2-sphere as made up of a sequence of 1-spheres (circles) which grow from a point and then contract to a point—for example, the circles of constant latitude. The initial point and final point are the north and south poles of the sphere.

Another way to describe these spheres is with pictures, at least for the low dimensionalities. By seeing how the low-dimensional spheres are related we can find constructions which enable us to go on to imagine the higher ones. Let us draw the first three:

0-sphere, actually two points　　　•　　•

1-sphere

2-sphere

These figures can be obtained recursively, at least so far as their topology or essential connectedness is concerned, by a construction called "suspension." We suspend the 0-sphere to obtain the 1-sphere, suspend the 1-sphere to obtain the 2-sphere, and so on. Suspension consists in adding two points to the figure, and then connecting these two points with all the points of the figure to be suspended (so that the original figure is "suspended" from the two points as if by strings). Suspend the o-sphere:

new points

Note that this is nothing less than a circle, if we just smooth it out. Suspend the 1-sphere:

new point

1-sphere

new point

The resulting figure is the 2-sphere if we just round it a little. Suspend the 2-sphere:

new point

One new point can go inside, and the suspending strings then fill up the 2-sphere to make a solid ball. The other new point has to go outside, but the suspending strings cannot be easily visualized without a kind of "cowlick," which is, in fact, *not* a property of the 3-sphere, but a defect of this method of visualizing it.

Finally we can obtain these spheres by gluing together cones, but with only one point, not two. That is, add *one* new point, and join this point to all the points of the figure to be "coned":

cone on the o-sphere

    glue

another cone on the o-sphere

This makes the 1-sphere. It is clear why it works: we are describing suspension, but in two steps, first forming the two cones, and second gluing them:

cone on the 1-sphere

    glue

another cone on the 1-sphere

The cone on the 2-sphere is a solid ball (put the new point inside):

glue

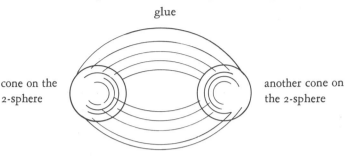

cone on the
2-sphere

another cone on
the 2-sphere

The "gluing" part is what is hard to visualize, but we need not *actually* visualize it if we just remember that corresponding points on the surfaces of the two balls are really the same and that we (like Dante) draw them twice only for convenience.

48. Singleton, *The Divine Comedy: Paradiso 2: Commentary,* p. 439.

49. The passage in full is as follows:

> E com'io mi rivolsi e furon tocchi
>   li miei da ciò che pare in quel volume,
>   quandunque nel suo giro ben s'adocchi,
> un punto vidi che raggiava lume
>   acuto sì, che 'l viso ch'elli affoca
>   chiuder conviensi per lo forte acume;
> e quale stella par quinci più poca,
>   parrebbe luna, locata con esso
>   come stella con stella si colloca.
> Forse cotanto quanto pare appresso
>   alo cigner la luce che 'l dipigne
>   quando 'l vapor che 'l porta più è spesso,
> distante intorno al punto un cerchio d'igne
>   si girava sì ratto, ch'avria vinto
>   quel moto che più tosto il mondo cigne;
> e questo era d'un altro circumcinto,
>   e quel dal terzo, e 'l terzo poi dal quarto,
>   dal quinto il quarto, e poi dal sesto il quinto.
> Sopra seguiva il settimo sì sparto
>   già di larghezza, che 'l messo di Iuno
>   intero a contenerlo sarebbe arto.
> Così l'ottavo e 'l nono; e ciascheduno
>   più tardo si movea, secondo ch'era
>   in numero distante più da l'uno;
> e quello avea la fiamma più sincera
>   cui men distava la favilla pura,
>   credo, però che più di lei s'invera.

And as I turned and my eyes were touched by what
appears in that volume, whenever in its turning one
spots it, I saw a point which radiated a light so
intense that the eye on which it blazes must close
for its strong in-sight; and whatever star seems
smallest from here would seem a moon if placed beside
it like a star with a neighboring star. Perhaps as
near as a halo seems to girdle the light which paints
it, when the vapor that bears it is most thick, at
such a distance around the point a circle of fire was
whirling so rapidly that it would have surpassed that
motion that most immediately girds the world; and
this was girt around by another and that by a third,
and the third by a fourth, by a fifth the fourth, then
by a sixth the fifth. Thereon followed the seventh so
wide that the messenger of Juno entire would be too
narrow to contain it. So the eighth and the ninth;
and each was moving more slowly according as it was in
number more distant from the one. And that one had the
purest flame which the pure spark is least distant from,
I believe, because the former intruths itself the most in
the latter. (*Par.* XXVIII, 13–39)

I have altered Singleton's translation slightly in an attempt to
preserve at least a few of the *double entendres* (*volume, acume*)
and neologisms (*s'invera*) by means of which Dante plays with
and upon his four-dimensional spatial imagery.

50. Freccero, "The Fig Tree and the Laurel," p. 38.
51. As far as I know Dante follows no theological tradition in carry-
ing the metamathematical process implied by the number three
from the third dimension to a fourth in *Paradiso* XXVIII. I would
argue that the higher mathematics of this canto lead to the conclusion that the significance he attaches to the number three is not
attributable *merely* to received tradition.
52. Thomas S. Kuhn, *The Structure of Scientific Revolutions,* International Encyclopedia of Unified Science, vol. 2, no. 2, 2nd ed.
(Chicago: The University of Chicago Press, 1970), see esp. pp.
1–9, 66–76, 174–210.
53. Roche, "The Calendrical Structure," p. 171.
54. Durling, *The Figure of the Poet in Renaissance Epic,* p. 84.
55. Joseph A. Barber, "Rhyme Scheme Patterns in Petrarch's *Canzoniere,*" *MLN* 92 (1977):146.
56. Paul de Man, "The Rhetoric of Temporality," in *Interpretation:
Theory and Practice,* ed. Charles S. Singleton (Baltimore: The
Johns Hopkins Press, 1969), p. 197.
57. Ibid., p. 197.
58. It becomes thematically clear in Sonnet 189 that the ironic con-

sciousness of error constitutes anything but a reversal of the disintegrative process, a significant point which de Man also makes in his argument. Cf. "Rhetoric of Temporality," p. 197.

59. Wilkins, *The Making of the "Canzoniere,"* pp. 150–53.
60. Aldo S. Bernardo, *Petrarch, Laura, and the "Triumphs"* (Albany, N.Y.: State University of New York Press, 1974), p. 28.
61. Wilkins, *The Making of the "Canzoniere,"* p. 352.
62. Here and elsewhere in this study, I am using the terms "figurative" and "figural" interchangeably, as contemporary usage and theoretical commentary suggest they may be. See esp. Paul de Man, *Allegories of Reading: Figural Language in Rousseau, Nietzsche, Rilke, and Proust* (New Haven and London: Yale University Press, 1979). In other words, I do not mean to restrict the sense of "figural" to Auerbach's "typological" discourse. Cf. Auerbach, "Figura."
63. Noferi, *L'esperienza poetica del Petrarca,* p. 73. English translation mine. Noferi writes, . . . *con un filo di progressione temporale continua e romanzata.*
64. De Man, "Rhetoric of Temporality," p. 197.
65. Punctuation of the first stanza of *Canzone* 23 varies from edition to edition. I follow Contini here. Zingarelli and Durling would place a semicolon rather than a period at the end of line six. As my reading of this stanza indicates, however, the relationships among clauses are indeterminate regardless of punctuation. The possibilities which editors have felt justified in choosing all observe the groupings of lines which I follow in my discussion. Cf. *Le rime di Francesco Petrarca,* con saggio introduttivo e commento di Nicola Zingarelli (Bologna: Zanichelli, 1964), p. 348.
66. For a complementary discussion of the role of memory in Sonnet 90, see Mazzotta, "The *Canzoniere* and the Language of the Self," p. 278.
67. Cf. Ponchiroli's notes in Contini, *Canzionere,* p. 26, and Zingarelli, *Le rime di Francesco Petrarca,* p. 349.
68. The relevance to Petrarch's poetics of this distinction, and of the relationship between the modes of discourse that the terms "figurative" and "performative" are used here to name, were first called to my attention by Timothy Bahti of the Department of Comparative Literature, Cornell University. Cf. de Man's characterization of a process of reading "in which rhetoric is a disruptive intertwining of trope and persuasion or—which is not quite the same thing—of cognitive and performative language" in *Allegories of Reading,* p. ix. Also a brilliantly argued reading of Shelley's "Triumph of Life" in which the notions of performance, figuration, and signification come to seem as complexly commented upon by the poem as they are useful in a commentary on it. See Paul de Man's "Shelley Disfigured" in Harold Bloom, et al., *Deconstruction and Criticism* (New York: The Seabury Press, 1979), esp. pp. 62–66.

69. Citations from Ovid are quoted from *Metamorphoses,* with a translation by Frank Justus Miller, The Loeb Classical Library, 2 vols. (Cambridge, Mass.: Harvard University Press, 1966). Translations are Miller's.

70. See Brenkman, "Narcissus in the Text," pp. 35–36, for a full theoretical discussion of this interpretation of Narcissus' narrative.

71. There is a subtle difference, however, between the *lauro* into which the poet is said to be transformed in *l.* 39 and the *alloro* which he has not been able to leave by the end of the poem (*l.* 167). The first term names a tree, the second, technically speaking, the kind of leaf that the tree produces. The two may well be operating as synecdoches for each other, but I think the change also admits of the reading that, like Narcissus, Petrarch's lover, as he disappears from his own history, reappears or is replaced by a poetic image. The laurel crown of the poet, which would be made up of the laurel leaves of the end of the poem, is comparable to the flower of Ovid's Narcissus story in the sense that each is a nondissimulating image or figure produced by but not coincident with a prior figure which is misleading. In the same sense that Narcissus' *flower* figures the purely rhetorical status of the figures that preceded it in the story Narcissus tells himself, so Petrarch's laurel *leaf* is a witty figure for the literary nature of the more substantial-seeming *lauro* it has grown out of. The special twist that Petrarch gives to the Ovidian motif is to make the final figure to all intents and purposes the *same* as the first, as if to imply that the only significant change which might occur over the course of the poem would have to occur in the mode of interpretation brought to bear on it.

72. The reading of the Narcissus passage which has been most suggestive for my reading of Dante's and Petrarch's Ovid is that of John Brenkman (see Brenkman, "Narcissus in the Text," pp. 7–59). Brenkman, however, tends to see his remarks as more derivative of his own theoretical approach than of Ovid's text.

Chapter III

1. Discussions of early commentaries on the *Trionfi* are to be found in the following volumes: Francesco Petrarca, *Trionfi,* Introduzione e note di Carlo Calcaterra (Torino: Unione Tipografico-editrice Torinese, 1927); D. D. Carnicelli, ed., *Lord Morley's Tryumphes of Fraunces Petrarcke* (Cambridge, Mass.: Harvard University Press, 1971), pp. 28–37; Ernest Hatch Wilkins, "The *Quattrocento* Editions of the *Canzoniere* and the Triumphs" and "The Separate Quattrocento Editions of the Triumphs," in *The Making of the "Canzoniere" and Other Petrarchan Studies* (Rome: Edizioni di storia e letteratura, 1951), pp. 379–413.

2. Quoted from Carnicelli, *Lord Morley's Tryumphes of Fraunces Petrarcke*, p. 36.
3. These issues were formulated for twentieth-century scholars by (Victor Massena) Prince d'Essling and Eugene Müntz in their comprehensive study, *Pétrarque, ses études d'art, son influence sur les artistes, ses portraits, et ceux de Laure, et l'illustration de ses écrits* (Paris: Gazette des Beaux Arts, 1902). One of the most recent and best articles dealing with the discrepancy between Petrarch's poem and its illustrations is that of Lynn White, Jr., "Indic Elements in the Iconography of Petrarch's 'Trionfo della morte,'" *Speculum* 49 (April 1974):201–21.
4. John Freccero, "Introduction," *The Paradiso: Dante's ultimate vision of universal harmony and eternal salvation,* trans. John Ciardi (New York: The New American Library, 1970), p. xiii.
5. Pierre de Nolhac, *Pétrarque et l'humanisme* (Paris: Librairie Honoré Champion, Editeur, 1907), pp. 156–58. De Nolhac lists several Roman histories among the annotations found in Petrarch's copy of the *Aeneid*. See also Paget Toynbee, *Dante Studies and Researches* (London, 1902), p. 113 for quotations from the *Magnae derivationes* of Ugoccione da Pisa, with whose accounts of Roman triumphs both Dante and Petrarch were well acquainted.
6. Francesco Petrarca, *Le rime di Francesco Petrarca,* con saggio introduttivo e commento di Nicola Zingarelli (Bologna: Zanichelli, 1964). In English, "Do not make an idol of a name, empty without subject" (*Rime* 128. 76–77).
7. All citations from Petrarch's *Trionfi* are quoted from Francesco Petrarca, *Rime, Trionfi e poesie latine,* ed. F. Neri, G. Martellotti, E. Bianchi, N. Sapegno (Milano, Napoli: Riccardo Ricciardi, editore, 1951). I abbreviate the titles of the *Trionfi* by using the first letters of the Latin titles: *"Triumphus cupidinis," "Triumphus pudicitie," "Triumphus mortis," "Triumphus fame," "Triumphus temporis," "Triumphus eternitatis."* English translations are my own. For a graceful but less literal translation of the entire *Trionfi* see *The Triumphs of Petrarch,* trans. Ernest Hatch Wilkins (Chicago: The University of Chicago Press, 1962).
8. Thomas G. Bergin, *Petrarch,* Twayne's World Authors Series, No. 81 (New York: Twayne Publishers, 1970), p. 152.
9. Umberto Bosco, *Petrarca* (Torino: Unione Tipografico-editrice Torinese, 1946), p. 237. All English translations of Bosco's text are mine. Here he writes, *Tralascio i paragoni di cui è gratificato l'avversario di lei, Amore. Tutto ciò per dire semplicemente che Amore tende il suo arco contro Laura.*
10. Bosco, *Petrarca,* p. 232. *Se qualche volta descrive, e avviene rarissimamente, è sempre il paesaggio di Valchiusa. . . .*
11. C. S. Lewis, *The Discarded Image* (Cambridge: Cambridge University Press, 1964), p. 199.
12. Ibid., p. 203.
13. For an interesting discussion of "encyclopedic narrative" as a genre

of central importance more generally in Western literature see Edward Mendelson, "Encyclopedic Narrative: From Dante to Pynchon," *MLN* 91 (1976):1267–75.

14. E. R. Curtius, *European Literature and the Latin Middle Ages,* trans. Willard R. Trask (New York and Evanston: Harper and Row, 1963), p. 365. Curtius, however, considers the number (over five hundred) unusually high with respect to earlier medieval works.

15. After formulating these speculations, I encountered Hans Robert Jauss' corroborating remarks on C. S. Lewis in the title essay of his *Alterität und Modernität der mittelalterlichen Litteratur—Gesammelte Aufsätze 1956–1976* (Munich: Wilhelm Fink Verlag, 1977), pp. 19–20.

16. Bergin, *Petrarch,* p. 153.

17. Ibid., p. 149.

18. Ibid.

19. Hans Baron misses this important distinction in arguing that because there are more Biblical figures in the definitive version of the *"Triumphus fame"* than in earlier versions, Petrarch's attitude toward Christian culture must have changed. Instead the successive versions of this *trionfo* make more pointed Petrarch's exclusion from the poem of specifically Christian doctrine. Cf. Hans Baron, *From Petrarch to Leonardo Bruni: Studies in Humanistic and Political Literature* (Chicago and London: The University of Chicago Press, 1968), pp. 27–28.

Bibliography

I. Editions of Petrarch

Petrarca, Francesco. *Canzoniere*. Edited by Gianfranco Contini and Daniele Ponchiroli. Torino: Einaudi, 1968.
———. *Le Familiare*. 4 vols. Edited by Vittorio Rossi. Florence: Sansoni, 1933–42.
———. *Opere di Petrarca*. Edited by Giovanni Ponte. Milan: E. Mursia and C., 1968.
———. *Le rime di Francesco Petrarca*. Edited by Nicola Zingarelli. Bologna: Zanichelli, 1964.
———. *Rime, Trionfi e poesie latine*. La letteratura italiana: storia e testi, vol. 6. Edited by F. Neri, G. Martellotti, E. Binachi, N. Sapegno. Milan, Naples: Riccardo Ricciardi, 1951.
———. *Trionfi*. Edited by Carlo Calcaterra. Torino: Unione Tipografico-editrice Torinese, 1927.

II. Translations of Petrarch

Petrarch's Lyric Poems. Translated by Robert M. Durling. Cambridge, Mass.: Harvard University Press, 1976.
Petrarch's Secret. Translated by William H. Draper. London: Chatto and Windus, 1811.
The Triumphs of Petrarch. Translated by Ernest Hatch Wilkins. Chicago: The University of Chicago Press, 1962.

III. Editions of Other Classical, Medieval, and Renaissance Texts

Anthology of the Provençal Troubadours. Edited by R. T. Hill and T. G. Bergin. 2nd ed., edited by Thomas Bergin, Susan Olson,

William Paden, Jr., Nathaniel Smith. New Haven: Yale University Press, 1973. Vol. 1.

Augustine. *On Christian Doctrine.* The Library of Liberal Arts, No. 80. Translated by D. W. Robertson, Jr. New York: The Liberal Arts Press, 1958.

Biblia Sacra. Vulgate Editionis Sixti V Pontificis Maximi et Clementis VIII Auctoritate Edita. Rome: Editiones Paulinae, 1957.

Dante Alighieri. *The Divine Comedy.* Bollingen Series LXXX. 6 vols. Translated by Charles S. Singleton. Princeton: Princeton University Press, 1970–75.

————. *La Vita Nuova.* Edited by Giovanni Melodia. Milano: Dottor Francesco Vallardi, 1905.

Lyrics of the Troubadours and Trouveres: An Anthology and a History. Translated by Frederick Goldin. New York: Anchor/Doubleday, 1973.

Ovid. *Metamorphoses.* Loeb Classical Library. 2 vols. Translated by Frank Justus Miller. Cambridge, Mass.: Harvard University Press, 1966.

Virgil. *Eclogues, Georgics, Aeneid.* Loeb Classical Library. 2 vols. Translated by H. R. Fairclough. Cambridge, Mass.: Harvard University Press, 1974.

IV. Critical Studies of Petrarch, Dante, and Medieval and Renaissance Topics

Amaturo, Raffaele. *Petrarca.* Roma-Bari: Editori Laterza, 1974.

Auerbach, Erich. "Figura." 1939. Reprint in *Scenes from the Drama of European Literature.* Translated by Ralph Manheim. New York: Meridian Books, 1959. Pp. 11–76.

Barber, Joseph A. "Rhyme Scheme Patterns in Petrarch's *Canzoniere.*" *MLN* 92 (1977):139–46.

Baron, Hans. *From Petrarch to Leonardo Bruni: Studies in Humanistic and Political Literature.* Chicago: The University of Chicago Press, 1968.

Bergin, Thomas G. *Petrarch.* Twayne's World Authors Series, No. 81. New York: Twayne Publishers, 1970.

Bernardo, Aldo S. *Petrarch, Laura, and the "Triumphs."* Albany, N.Y.: State University of New York Press, 1974.

Bosco, Umberto. *Petrarca.* Torino: Unione Tipografico-editrice Torinese, 1946.

Brenkman, John Preston. "Narcissus in the Text: Toward an Analysis of the Literary Subject in Ovid, Petrarch, and Yeats." Dissertation, The University of Iowa, 1974.

Burckhardt, Jacob. *The Civilization of the Renaissance in Italy.* 2nd ed. 1868. Translated by S. G. C. Middlemore. Reprint. New York: The New American Library of World Literature, 1960.

Calcaterra, Carlo. *Nella selva del Petrarca*. Bologna: Editore Licinio Cappelli, 1942.

Cambon, Glauco. *Dante's Craft: Studies in Language and Style*. Minneapolis: The University of Minnesota Press, 1969.

Carnicelli, D. D. "Introduction." In *Lord Morley's Tryumphes of Fraunces Petrarcke*. Edited by D. D. Carnicelli. Cambridge, Mass.: Harvard University Press, 1971. Pp. 3–74.

Cosenza, Mario Emilio. *Francesco Petrarca and the Revolution of Cola di Rienzo*. Chicago: The University of Chicago Press, 1913.

Curtius, E. R. *European Literature and the Latin Middle Ages*. Translated by Willard R. Trask. New York and Evanston: Harper and Row, 1963.

Dragonetti, Roger. "The Double Play of Arnaut Daniel's *Sestina* and Dante's *Divina Commedia*." *Yale French Studies* 55/56 (1977): 227–52.

Durling, Robert M. "The Ascent of Mt. Ventoux and the Crisis of Allegory." *Italian quarterly* 18, 69 (Summer 1974):7–28.

———. *The Figure of the Poet in Renaissance Epic*. Cambridge, Mass.: Harvard University Press, 1965.

D'Essling, Prince (Victor Massena) and Eugene Müntz. *Pétrarque, ses études d'art, son influence sur les artistes, ses portraits, et ceux de Laure, et l'illustration de ses écrits*. Paris: Gazette des Beaux Arts, 1902.

Foscolo, Ugo. *Essays on Petrarch*. London: John Murray, 1823.

Freccero, John. "The Fig Tree and the Laurel: Petrarch's Poetics." *Diacritics* 5, 1 (1975):34–40.

———. "Introduction." In *The Paradiso: Dante's ultimate vision of universal harmony and eternal salvation*. Translated by John Ciardi. New York: The New American Library, 1970. Pp. ix–xxi.

Giudici, Giovanni. "Signor Petrarca, permette che la intervisti?" *L'Espresso* 18 (5 May 1974).

Greene, Thomas. "Petrarch and the Humanist Hermeneutic." In *Italian Literature, Roots and Branches: Essays in Honor of Thomas Godard Bergin*. Edited by Giose Rimanelli and Kenneth John Achity. New Haven: Yale University Press, 1976. Pp. 201–24.

Jauss, Hans Robert. *Alterität und Modernität der mittelalterlichen Literatur—Gesammelte Aufsätze 1956–1976*. Munich: Wilhelm Fink Verlag, 1977.

Lewis, C. S. *The Discarded Image*. Cambridge: Cambridge University Press, 1964.

Mazzotta, Giuseppe. "The *Canzoniere* and the Language of the Self." *Studies in Philology* 75, 3 (Summer 1978):271–96.

———. *Dante, Poet of the Desert*. Princeton: Princeton University Press, 1979.

———. "Poetics of History: Inferno XXVI." *Diacritics* 5, 2 (1975): 37–44.

Mommsen, Theodor E. "Petrarch's Conception of the 'Dark Ages.'" *Speculum* 17 (April 1942):226–42.

Newman, Francis X. "St. Augustine's Three Visions and the Structure of the *Commedia.*" *MLN* 82 (1967):56–78.

Noferi, Adelia. *L'esperienza poetica del Petrarca.* Firenze: Felice le Monier, 1962.

Nolhac, Pierre de. *Pétrarque et l'humanisme.* Paris: Librairie Honoré Champion, Editeur, 1907.

Peterson, Mark. "Dante and the 3-sphere." *American Journal of Physics* 47, 12 (December 1979):1031–35.

Phelps, Ruth Shepard. *The Earlier and Later Forms of Petrarch's "Canzoniere."* Chicago: The University of Chicago Press, 1925.

Roche, Thomas, Jr. "The Calendrical Structure of Petrarch's *Canzoniere.*" *Studies in Philology* 71, 2 (1974):152–72.

Scaglione, Aldo. "La struttura del *Canzoniere* e il metodo di composizione del Petrarca." *Lettere Italiane* 27, 5 (1975):129–39.

Singleton, Charles S. *Commedia: Elements of Structure.* Dante Studies I. Cambridge, Mass · Harvard University Press, 1954.

Sturm, Sara. "The Poet-Persona in the *Canzoniere.*" In *Francis Petrarch, Six Centuries Later: A Symposium.* North Carolina Studies in the Romance Languages and Literatures: Symposia, 3. Edited by Aldo Scaglione. Chapel Hill and Chicago: Department of Romance Languages, University of North Carolina and The Newberry Library, 1975. Pp. 192–212.

Toynbee, Paget. *Dante Studies and Researches.* London: Methuen & Co., 1902.

Trinkaus, Charles. *"In Our Image and Likeness."* 2 vols. London: Constable and Co., 1970.

———. *The Poet as Philosopher: Petrarch and the Formation of Renaissance Consciousness.* New Haven: Yale University Press, 1979.

White, Lynn, Jr. "Indic Elements in the Iconography of Petrarch's 'Trionfi della morte.'" *Speculum* 49 (April 1974):201–21.

Wilkins, Ernest Hatch. *The Making of the "Canzoniere" and Other Petrarchan Studies.* Rome: Edizioni di storia e letteratura, 1951.

V. Theoretical and Critical Discussions of Literature and Related Human Sciences

Barthes, Roland. "To Write: Intransitive Verb?" In *The Structuralist Controversy: The Languages of Criticism and the Sciences of Man.* Edited and translated by Richard Macksey and Eugenio Donato. Baltimore: The Johns Hopkins University Press, 1972. Pp. 134–56.

Bloom, Harold. *The Anxiety of Influence: A Theory of Poetry.* New York: Oxford University Press, 1973.

———. *A Map of Misreading.* New York: Oxford University Press, 1975.

———. *Wallace Stevens: The Poems of Our Climate.* Ithaca, N.Y.: Cornell University Press, 1977.

Derrida, Jacques. *De la grammatologie*. Paris: Les Editions de Minuit, 1967.

———. *La dissémination*. Paris: Editions du Seuil, 1972.

———. *L'écriture et la différence*. Paris: Editions du Seuil, 1967.

———. "Structure, Sign, and Play in the Discourse of the Human Sciences." In *The Structuralist Controversy: The Languages of Criticism and the Sciences of Man*. Edited and translated by Richard Macksey and Eugenio Donato. Baltimore: The Johns Hopkins University Press, 1972. Pp. 247–72.

Eco, Umberto. "The poetics of an open work." Translated by Bruce Merry. In *Twentieth Century Studies: The Limits of Comprehension*. Edinburgh, Scotland: Scottish Academic Press Limited, 1974. Pp. 6–26.

Fiedler, Leslie. *No! in Thunder: Essays on Myth and Literature*. Boston: Beacon Press, 1960.

Kuhn, Thomas S. *The Structure of Scientific Revolutions*. International Encyclopedia of Unified Science, vol. 2, no. 2, 2nd ed. Chicago: The University of Chicago Press, 1970.

Man, Paul de. *Allegories of Reading: Figural Language in Rousseau, Nietzsche, Rilke, and Proust*. New Haven and London: Yale University Press, 1979.

———. *Blindness and Insight: Essays in the Rhetoric of Contemporary Criticism*. New York: Oxford University Press, 1971.

———. "The Rhetoric of Temporality." In *Interpretation: Theory and Practice*. Edited by Charles S. Singleton. Baltimore: The Johns Hopkins University Press, 1969. Pp. 173–209.

———. "Shelley Disfigured." In *Deconstruction and Criticism*. Bloom, et al. New York: The Seabury Press, 1979. Pp. 39–73.

Mendelson, Edward. "Encyclopedic Narrative: From Dante to Pynchon." *MLN* 91 (1976): 1267–75.

Mitchell, Juliet. *Psychoanalysis and Feminism*. 1974. Reprint. New York: Vintage, 1975.

White, Hayden. "The Problem of Change in Literary History." *New Literary History* 7 (1975):97–111.

Index

Library of Congress Cataloging in Publication Data
Waller, Marguerite R   1948-
Petrarch's poetics and literary history.
Bibliography: p.
Includes index.
1. Petrarca, Francesco, 1304-1374—Versification.
2. Petrarca, Francesco, 1304-1374—Style.   I. Title.
PQ4541.W3   851'.1   80-12893
ISBN 0-87023-305-X